D1550641

UGANDA
in Pictures

Eric Braun

Twenty-First Century Books

Contents

Website address: www.lernerbooks.com

Twenty-First Century Books
A division of Lerner Publishing Group
241 First Avenue North
Minneapolis, MN 55401 U.S.A.

web enhanced @ www.vgsbooks.com

CULTURAL LIFE 46

▶ Religion and Holidays. The Media and the Arts. Language and Literature. Clothing. Food. Sports and Recreation.

THE ECONOMY 58

▶ Agriculture. Services. Industry. Transportation and Telecommunications. The Future.

FOR MORE INFORMATION

Library of Congress Cataloging-in-Publication Data

Braun, Eric, 1971-
        Uganda in pictures / by Eric Braun.
            p.   cm. — (Visual geography series)
        Includes bibliographical references and index.
        ISBN-13: 978-0-8225-2397-0 (lib. bdg. : alk. paper)
        ISBN-10: 0-8225-2397-3 (lib. bdg. : alk. paper)
        1. Uganda—Juvenile literature. 2. Uganda—Pictorial works—Juvenile literature. I. Title. II. Visual
geography series (Minneapolis, Minn.)
DT433.222.B75 2006
967.61—dc22   2005009963

Manufactured in the United States of America
1 2 3 4 5 6 - BP - 11 10 09 08 07 06

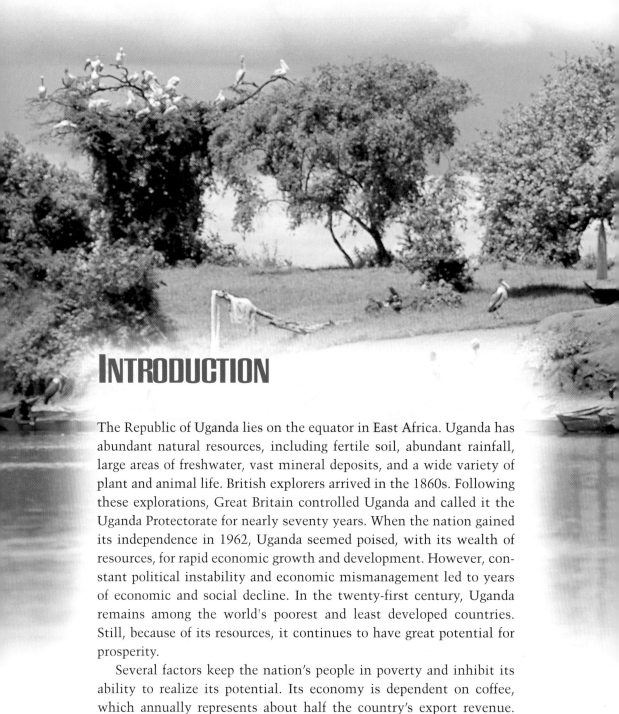

INTRODUCTION

The Republic of Uganda lies on the equator in East Africa. Uganda has abundant natural resources, including fertile soil, abundant rainfall, large areas of freshwater, vast mineral deposits, and a wide variety of plant and animal life. British explorers arrived in the 1860s. Following these explorations, Great Britain controlled Uganda and called it the Uganda Protectorate for nearly seventy years. When the nation gained its independence in 1962, Uganda seemed poised, with its wealth of resources, for rapid economic growth and development. However, constant political instability and economic mismanagement led to years of economic and social decline. In the twenty-first century, Uganda remains among the world's poorest and least developed countries. Still, because of its resources, it continues to have great potential for prosperity.

Several factors keep the nation's people in poverty and inhibit its ability to realize its potential. Its economy is dependent on coffee, which annually represents about half the country's export revenue.

But the price of coffee fluctuates, creating an unstable economy. The needs of a rapidly growing population, to which an ever-increasing number of refugees contribute, strain Uganda's society. Rebel, antigovernment groups, particularly the Lord's Resistance Army (LRA), wreak violence and terror on people in parts of the rural north. And disease, especially AIDS (acquired immunodeficiency syndrome), victimizes people from all parts of society.

Uganda is home to dozens of ethnic groups. Historically, the country has experienced deep ethnic divisions among these groups. Broadly speaking, the country can be divided between the mostly rural northern and the more urban southern regions. Throughout history, social and political power has been concentrated in the southern region, especially within the kingdom of Buganda. Even when Uganda came under British control, special treatment and power was granted to Buganda, inflaming ethnic tensions that were already high due to years of competition for power and influence.

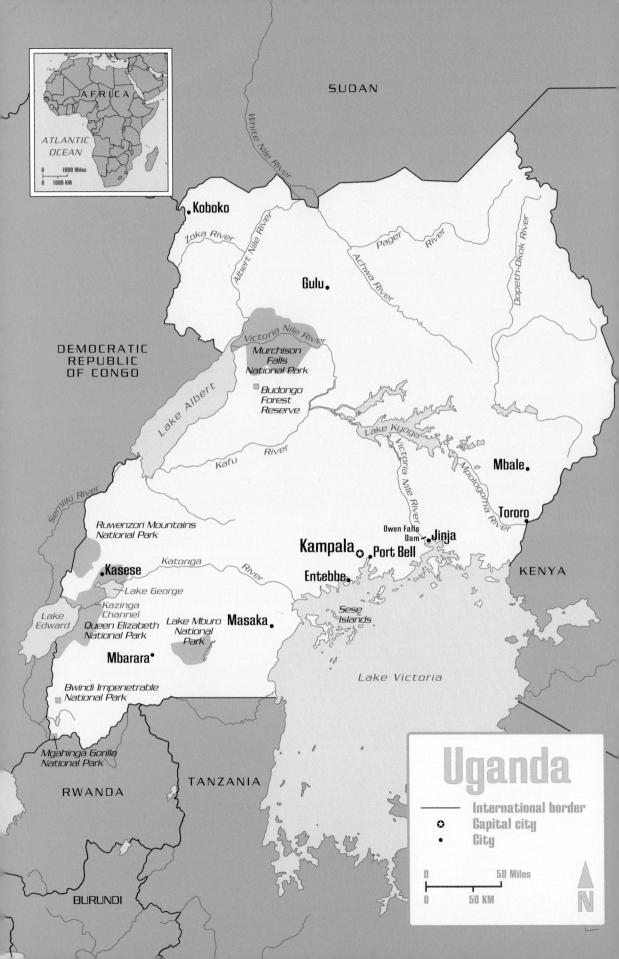

After independence, dictators (leaders who rule with complete personal control), including Idi Amin, poured vast amounts of money into the military and terrorized the people. The power of Buganda was stripped away, angering the country's most numerous and prosperous people. Civil war ravaged the country for two decades until 1986, when Yoweri Museveni and his National Resistance Army (NRA) seized power. Museveni has remained in power longer than any previous Ugandan leader. He has managed to restore relative peace and a small degree of prosperity to Uganda. Even ethnic tensions have been reduced.

Winston Churchill, a former British prime minister, published a book called *My African Journey* in 1908. He praised Uganda's beauty and variety, saying, "Uganda is truly the pearl of Africa." Yet throughout the second half of the twentieth century, the country was one of the most violent and poorest in the world. In the twenty-first century, its challenges remain immense, but progress has been made in recent years to reduce them. Due to a vigorous prevention program, the rate of AIDS infection has dropped from 30 percent to 5 percent. The economy is gradually growing stronger. More children are going to school. And with its fertile land and hardworking people, the country grows enough food to feed its people. Ugandans work to continue to return the luster to the pearl.

THE LAND

The Republic of Uganda is located in east central Africa, a part of the African continent that, along with Kenya and Tanzania, is known as East Africa. Compared to many African nations, Uganda is small at 93,066 square miles (241,040 square kilometers)—about the size of the U.S. state of Oregon. But its diversity in landscape and life-forms is remarkable for an area its size. Its elevation (height above sea level) ranges from a low of about 2,000 feet (610 meters) to a peak of 16,762 feet (5,109 m). Uganda lies on the equator, the midpoint on earth between the North Pole and the South Pole, and 18 percent of its area is covered by freshwater lakes and rivers. For these reasons, this nation is home to both glacial (extremely cold) and tropical (warm and wet) areas, rain forests (tropical woodlands that receive plentiful rain year-round), and even semideserts, which suffer frequent drought. The plants and animals that live in Uganda are as varied as its environments.

Most of the country is a flat stretch of elevated land called a plateau, between 3,000 and 6,000 feet (914 and 1,829 m) above sea level. The

plateau is roughly circle-shaped, draining toward Lake Kyoga in its center. Mountain ranges circle Uganda and form a rim around the basin.

The nation is bordered on the east by Kenya and Lake Victoria, and on the south by Tanzania. To the southwest lies Rwanda, and to the west is the Democratic Republic of Congo (DRC), or Congo. Sudan borders Uganda to the north. The Indian Ocean, the ocean nearest to Uganda, is 500 miles (800 km) beyond the Kenyan border to the east.

Uganda is known as the Cradle of the Nile because its southeastern border cuts through Lake Victoria, the lake where the world's longest river, the Nile, begins. Lake Victoria, the world's second-largest freshwater lake (after North America's Lake Superior), contains parts of Uganda's borders with Kenya and Tanzania to the south.

Topography

The topography (physical features) of East Africa has been shaped by violent earth movements, mainly between 11,500 and 2 million ago. These earth shifts lifted up the plateau on which Uganda lies and later created the hills that characterize much of it. These earth shifts also created the mountains that surround the plateau. Uganda has four distinct topographical regions: the mountain regions, the Great Rift Valley, the Central Plateau, and the Lake Victoria region.

The mountain regions are found along the eastern and western borders of the country. In the east stands Mount Elgon, a dormant volcano on the country's border with Kenya. It is the second-tallest mountain in Uganda at 14,177 feet (4,321 m) above sea level, with ridges radiating from its crater for 19 miles (30 km). Kadam Peak (10,020 feet or 3,054 m high) is north of Mount Elgon near the Kenya border. Mount Moroto, at 10,121 feet (3,085 m), is north of that. In the northeast, Mount Zulia, Mount Morungole, and the Labwor and Dodoth Hills reach heights greater than 6,500 feet (2,000 m). A semidesert lies in the extreme northeast. The lower Imatong Mountains and Mount Langia (9,938 feet or 3,029 m) stand at the border with Sudan.

The Ruwenzori Mountains make up the most dramatic region of the western border. Known to early traders from the Middle East as the Mountains of the Moon, a name that is still used, these tall mountains make up about 50 miles (80 km) of Uganda's border with Congo. Even though the mountains lie on the equator, the highest peaks of the Ruwenzoris are cold and snowcapped, because air temperature drops as elevation rises. The highest mountain in the range is Mount Stanley, with its highest point, Margherita Peak, at 16,762 feet (5,109 m). Mount Stanley's Alexandra Peak is 16,677 feet (5,083 m) high.

Eight individual peaks on **Mount Stanley** have names. From the tallest to the lowest peak, they are Margherita, Alexandra, Albert, Savoia, Elena, Elizabeth, Phillip, and Moebius. The tallest two lie on Uganda's border with the Democratic Republic of Congo.

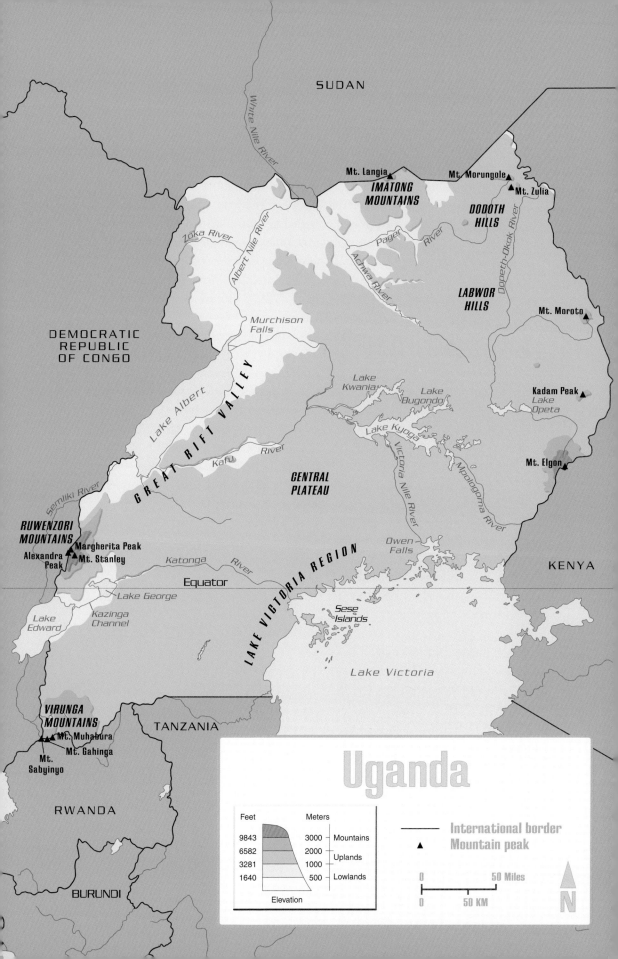

Farther south in the mountain region, in the extreme southwest corner of Uganda, three extinct volcanoes are part of the Virunga Mountains, most of which lie in Congo. The easternmost of the three mountains is Mount Muhabura. At 13,540 feet (4,127 m), it is the highest of the three. To the west of Muhabura is Mount Gahinga, also with a single cone. Mount Sabyinyo, with its double-cone peak, is the westernmost of the three. On its western cone, the boundaries of Uganda, Rwanda, and Congo meet. The boundaries of Uganda and Rwanda run along the summits of Muhabura and Gahinga. Other volcanoes in the Virunga range are active and dangerous.

PLATE TECTONICS

Scientists explain the formation of the Great Rift Valley with the theory of plate tectonics. This theory also explains earthquakes and volcanoes. According to this theory, the earth has an outer shell made up of about thirty rigid pieces called tectonic plates. The plates move around very slowly—at speeds up to about 4 inches (10 centimeters) per year. But the plates have been moving for hundreds of millions of years.

As the plates move, their boundaries may collide, spread apart, or slide alongside one another. When plates spread apart, it is called rifting. The western branch of the Great Rift Valley, on the western edge of Uganda, is in an early stage of rifting. Scientists expect that in about 50 million years, it will be filled with water from the Indian Ocean.

The western branch of the Great Rift Valley—a series of massive valleys that extends about 4,500 miles (7,200 km) through much of Asia and Africa—lies just east of the Ruwenzori Mountains in the west. Rain forests cover the foothills of the Ruwenzoris. The Great Rift Valley region contains the Lake Edward flats, occupied by Lakes Edward and George, where volcanic features such as craters and hot springs are common. Lake Albert to the north, where the section of the Nile River called the Albert Nile arises, is also part of the valley and is the lowest point in Uganda.

The relatively flat Central Plateau region forms the center of the country. Most of the plateau is about 4,000 feet (1,200 m) above sea level. The land slopes gently downward toward its center at Lake Kyoga. The land around Lake Kyoga is characterized by swamps and rivers and lakes. In the west, uplands rise from the flats near Lake Kyoga.

The Budongo Forest Reserve, an extensive mahogany forest, lies west of the lake. The northern half of the plateau is a vast savanna (open grasslands), drier than the land around the lakes.

The Nile River pours through a 21-foot (7-m) gap in the rocks and falls 120 feet (40 m) to form the **Murchison Falls** in Uganda's Murchison Falls National Park. For links to photographs of and more information about Uganda's national parks, geography, flora, and fauna, go to www.vgsbooks.com.

The Lake Victoria region makes up the southeastern part of the country. Rain forests lie on the western and northern shores of Lake Victoria. Off the northern shore, wide valleys separate a series of flat-topped hills. The soil is rich and the rain is plentiful, and much of the nation's coffee grows here. Kampala, the nation's capital and main commercial center, is in this region.

Lakes and Rivers

Nearly one-fifth of Uganda's area is covered in water. The massive Lake Victoria, in the southeastern corner of the country, is the headwaters, or beginning, of the Nile River. This southern section of the Nile, known as the Victoria Nile, flows from south to north. The lush Sese Islands in Lake Victoria are within Uganda's borders and attract tourists.

Lake Kyoga and several smaller lakes connected to it, known as finger lakes, dominate the central part of Uganda. These include Lake Kwania, Lake Bugondo, and Lake Opeta. All the lakes in the Lake Kyoga basin are shallow, usually reaching depths of only 30 feet (9 m). Lake Edward and Lake Albert lie along the western border with Congo.

The Victoria Nile River leaves Lake Victoria at Owen Falls near the city of Jinja and flows northwestward to form Lake Kyoga. North of Lake Kyoga, the Nile is joined by the Kafu River from the west. The river then flows over the spectacular Murchison Falls before flowing into Lake Albert. Flowing north from Lake Albert, the river is called the Albert Nile as it travels to the Sudan border. At Sudan it becomes the White Nile.

The Katonga River flows westward from Lake Victoria to Lake George. Lake George and Lake Edward are connected by a river called the Kazinga Channel. Flowing north from Lake Edward to Lake Albert is the Semliki River. It forms a part of Uganda's border with Congo. Other major rivers include the Zoka River in the northwest, the Achwa River in the north, the Pager River and the Dopeth-Okok River in the northeast, and the Mpologoma River in the southeast.

Climate

Lying on the equator, Uganda has a tropical climate (high temperatures and plentiful rainfall) that does not vary greatly during the year. However, because of Uganda's elevation, temperatures are milder there than in other tropical locations. In the mountainous regions, temperatures can get quite cool, with freezing temperatures (below 32°F, or 0°C) on the peaks of the Ruwenzoris. In most areas of the country, however, the temperature rarely goes below 60°F (16°C) or above 85°F (29°C). The hottest time of year is from December to February.

Most areas of Uganda have distinct wet and dry seasons. In much of the southern half, heavy rainfall occurs from March to May and from September to November. The area around Lake Victoria is the wettest part of the country. It receives substantial rainfall year-round. The greatest average annual rainfall in the nation occurs on the Sese Islands of Lake Victoria. They receive about 80 inches (200 centimeters) a year.

The northeastern part of Uganda is drier than the rest of the country. Its rainy season is April to August. Annual rainfall in that area averages about 20 inches (50 cm). In the rest of northern Uganda, the two rainy seasons overlap and last from April to October.

Natural Resources

Uganda has significant natural resources. The favorable climate, abundant water, and fertile soil allow the country to feed its population and grow crops, especially coffee, to sell. People herd cattle in the north, where the climate is too dry for many crops. Lakes, including Lake Victoria, the world's second-largest freshwater lake, supply fish for food and export. Water also supplies the country with power, as the Owen Falls Dam harnesses the force of rushing water at its hydroelectric plant. Uganda has rich mineral deposits, though only copper is mined on a large scale. Cobalt, nickel, and gold have been found in the west. The tourist industry taps the nation's beautiful scenery, friendly people, and wild animals to attract visitors to Uganda. Vast national parks draw visitors and help preserve endangered animals (animals threatened with extinction).

◎ Flora and Fauna

Plant life in Uganda is diverse, abundant, and lush. The ash of earlier volcanoes creates fertile soil that provides many nutrients for growing plants, and much of the country gets heavy rainfall. However, people have cut down trees to make farmlands and pastures where animals can graze, resulting in large areas where all vegetation has been cleared. Still, Uganda has rich flora (plant life). About 70 percent of the nation's area consists of dense forests, less dense woodland, and open grasslands.

Vegetation is heaviest in the south, where there are three main forest areas—two rain forests around the northern and western shores of Lake Victoria and a third forest on the mountains northeast of Lake Victoria. Cactus and thorny acacia trees grow in the northern part of the country, but grasses are the most common wild vegetation there. On the shores of Uganda's lakes, reeds and papyrus plants are common.

Banana plants are among the most important plants of Uganda, as they provide the nation's main food crop. From bananas, people also make alcoholic drinks including beer, and even clothing. Trees include plantain, fig, passion fruit, and mango. Other plants, such as corn, cassava (a starchy root), sweet potatoes, and peanuts (called groundnuts) are raised for food. Cotton grows wild in much of the country and is an important cash crop, sold to raise money. Other important cash crops are coffee and tea. These grow well in mountainous areas.

Bicyclists deliver bananas in Tororo, Uganda. **Bananas** are the main food source for many Ugandans. It takes nine months for a banana fruit to form. They grow in clusters called hands. Five hands of bananas are on each stem, or branch, of the banana plant. Individual bananas are called fingers. There are ten to twenty fingers per hand.

The crowned crane is the only crane to sit in trees. It likes isolated trees best for a full view of its world. These cranes usually fly with their legs stretched out behind them, but in cold weather, they will hold their feet beneath their breast feathers to keep them warm.

Fauna, or animal life, in Uganda is also diverse. The galago, or bush baby, is the smallest primate (mammals that includes humans and monkeys) in Africa. Many species of monkeys live in Uganda. So do chimpanzees, the closest living relative to humans. Elephants were poached (hunted illegally) nearly to extinction, but their numbers are increasing. They and another large mammal, the African buffalo, live in the west and north. Several species of antelope live in Uganda in large numbers. Other mammals include zebras, giraffes, lions, leopards, and hyenas. The rock hyrax is common all over. It is a hoofed animal whose closest relative is the elephant, though it looks something like a large guinea pig. Scientists think that a few highly endangered black rhinoceroses live in northern Uganda.

Lakes and rivers provide homes for hippopotamuses and crocodiles, including the Nile crocodile, which can grow to 16 feet (5 m) in length. Uganda also holds a vast variety of lizards, frogs, toads, and fish, such as ngege, tiger fish, and perch. Birds are also abundant, with more than one thousand known species in the country. The common bulbul and the mousebird are found everywhere. Herons, storks, and kingfishers are common around Lake Victoria. Vultures, hawks, eagles, and falcons live in the woodlands and grasslands. Uganda's national bird is the crowned crane. Insects, including disease-carrying mosquitoes and tsetse flies, are also abundant in Uganda.

Environmental Concerns

Many years of civil war, habitat destruction, and unchecked poaching destroyed much of Uganda's wildlife during the 1970s. Gradually wildlife is recovering. The country has a well-established system of national parks to protect wild animals and plants. Some of the world's most endangered animals live here, such as the mountain gorilla.

These are the largest of the great apes, with adult males weighing up to 240 pounds (110 kilograms). Despite their fearsome appearance, they are mostly gentle plant eaters. Only about an estimated six hundred mountain gorillas remain in the world. Most of them live in Uganda's Virunga Mountains, with some in Rwanda and Congo. The best place to view them, which requires a permit and a long trek with park guides, is the Bwindi Impenetrable National Park.

Deforestation, the loss of forests due to cutting down trees for fuel or timber or to clear land for agriculture, is another challenge. Removing trees, whose roots hold the soil in place, and grazing too many animals on land can lead to soil erosion. Wetlands are also drained for agriculture, leading to the loss of natural habitats (places where animals and plants live).

Female **mountain gorillas** have their first baby when they are about ten years old. They have just one baby at a time every three to four years, and in the wild they live for about forty years.

Trees flourish in the central business district of **Kampala,** Uganda.

◉ Cities

Only about 12 percent of Ugandans live in urban areas, but the number of urban dwellers is growing. Large numbers of younger people, mostly men, come to towns and cities seeking work. Most urban centers, including Kampala, the nation's largest city, are in the southern half of the country.

KAMPALA Founded off the shore of Lake Victoria in 1890 by a British explorer, Kampala (Hill of Antelopes) started out as a fort on a hill. The city became the nation's capital in 1962 and houses government buildings. Until 1971 it was known as one of the most beautiful, hospitable cities in the world. But that year, a military coup (sudden overthrow of the government) triggered a period of neglect, mismanagement, war, and destruction that turned Kampala into a shell of a city.

Peace and stability returned in 1986, and since then, the city has expanded to twenty hills. During the 1990s, it underwent a transformation as people removed war debris and rebuilt war-damaged structures. People also built new shops, hotels, office buildings, places of worship, parks, theaters, and nightclubs.

In modern Kampala, red-tiled mansions and green-roofed cottages sit next to tall, modern city buildings, with the countryside and Lake Victoria visible from the top of any of the hills. The palace of the kings of Buganda (a former kingdom of Uganda) stands on top of one of the hills. The population of Kampala is about 1.2 million people.

JINJA With about 100,000 people, Jinja is the second-largest city in Uganda. Only 50 miles (80 km) east of Kampala, Jinja also lies on the shores of Lake Victoria. In 1858 British explorer John Hanning Speke became the first European to reach Lake Victoria when he arrived at Jinja. He claimed that the Nile River began its journey here, a claim that geographers later confirmed. In 1954 the Owen Falls Dam on the Nile was opened and with it the hydroelectric plant. It uses the power of rushing water to generate electricity for most of Uganda and parts of Kenya.

The city is home to many cultures and has Asian, British, and indigenous (native) architecture. An important commercial and industrial center, it is home to many of the country's manufacturers because of its good supplies of water, power, land, and labor.

ENTEBBE is also on the shores of Lake Victoria, about 21 miles (34 km) south of Kampala. It is built on several small hills that slope down toward the lake, providing a view of the water from almost everywhere in the town. The city was founded in the nineteenth century, when British colonists built their administrative capital there. Entebbe was the capital of British-controlled Uganda and remained the capital until 1962, when the nation won its independence and the capital was moved to Kampala. However, a number of government offices still remain in Entebbe. The population of this town is about 90,500. Many residents work and shop in Kampala.

In 1976 Entebbe, Uganda, gained worldwide attention. That year Palestinian and German terrorists hijacked an Air France plane on its way from Athens, Greece, to Paris, France, and forced it to land in Entebbe. The terrorists demanded ransom money, as well as freedom for some of their compatriots, who were being held in Israeli jails. A group of Israeli commandos (a military unit specially trained for surprise raids) flew into the Entebbe airport, shot the hijackers, and rescued the travelers.

OTHER CITIES Other big cities in Uganda include Mbale (71,000 people) and Masaka (67,800 people). Accurate population statistics for Gulu, the only major city not located in the southern half of the country, are not available. Estimates range from 70,000 to 120,000 people. Rebel activity in the vicinity causes the displacement of large numbers of people.

HISTORY AND GOVERNMENT

Anthropologists (scientists who study human beings) believe that the first human beings *(Homo sapiens)* lived between 140,000 and 290,000 years ago in East Africa, including Uganda. Early peoples lived as hunter-gatherers. By the fourth century B.C., humans in Uganda had formed small villages and farms. The mild climate and reliable rainfall around Lake Victoria—an area that was covered in dense rain forest— made the area attractive to farmers, hunter-gatherers, and livestock herders. The country was divided into two groups, the Nilotic-speaking northerners and the Bantu-speaking southerners.

The Bantu-speaking people were farmers and also skilled at making iron weapons and tools. The Bantu-speakers migrated slowly until they populated most of Africa south of the Sahara Desert (sub-Saharan Africa). Their small societies around the Lake Victoria basin were organized into clans, small groups of people related by a common ancestor and run by clan chiefs. But eventually these societies grew too large for clan government. By around A.D. 1000, Nilotic-speaking

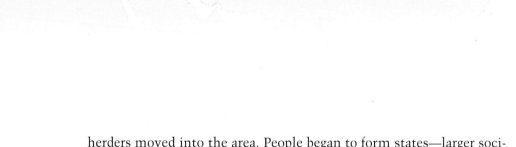

herders moved into the area. People began to form states—larger societies with more organized government. Over the next several hundred years, four main kingdoms emerged from these states.

The Four Kingdoms

Bunyoro-Kitara was the first state to form in Uganda. It was in the west-central part of the modern-day country. By about 1350, the state had a multilevel government controlled by a king. Revolts and struggles for power broke out, and by the end of the 1300s, part of Bunyoro's population fled the kingdom. They joined with people from the northeast to form a second kingdom, Buganda. Buganda was in the southern part of modern Uganda, around Lake Victoria. Its first kabaka, or king, was Kintu (who ruled from 1395 to 1408).

In the early 1400s, the third kingdom, the Ankole, formed in the western part of the country. This kingdom consisted of two groups: Hima herders were the ruling group, with the farming Ira people

The Kasubi Royal Tombs are a protected, 75-acre (30-hectare) UNESCO World Heritage Site in Kampala. Muzibu Azaala Mpanga, the central building, houses the tombs of four kabakas of Buganda. Though built in the 1880s, construction on the site used centuries-old Bagandan building techniques.

having less power and wealth. After Ankole's first king, Ruhinda, died in about 1446, the kingdom experienced a great deal of instability as several clans fought for control.

Meanwhile, the Bito, an aggressive group from southeastern Sudan, took over as the ruling dynasty (family in power) of Bunyoro-Kitara around 1500. Under Bito rule, the kingdom expanded its territory and dominated the region, establishing an empire with subdynasties. Buganda, too, began to expand its power. During the reign of Kabaka Katerega, from 1636 to 1663, Buganda more than doubled its size. In the 1700s, Ankole began its own period of expansion.

A fourth important kingdom, Toro, was established in about 1830. Prince Kaboyo established Toro in western Uganda, after he learned that he would not succeed to the Bunyoro-Kitara throne. Kaboyo then defeated an army sent by his father, who wanted to crush the new kingdom.

By the mid-nineteenth century, Buganda had doubled its territory again. Chiefs nominated by the kabaka governed its conquered lands. Buganda had become the most powerful kingdom in the region, and it sought to destroy Bunyoro-Kitara's remaining influence.

The Outside World Comes In

Uganda remained relatively isolated from the rest of the world until the middle of the nineteenth century, when outsiders began to arrive. Coastal ivory traders (ivory comes from elephant tusks) began working farther and farther inland from the Indian Ocean. People also traded slaves. Slaves were captured in the interior of Africa and then sold on the market alongside ivory. In the early years of the slave trade, slaves were sold mainly to buyers in the Middle East. But by the late 1700s, the African slave trade grew quickly as thousands of slaves were sent to plantations (large farms) all over the world.

Firearms were becoming more effective, and elephant herds near the coast had become nearly exterminated. Large caravans (traveling groups) of Arab traders reached Lake Victoria by 1844. Trade routes gradually extended into Buganda and Bunyoro-Kitara and parts of northern Uganda. These traders introduced guns, as well as the religion of Islam, to Uganda.

The search for the headwaters of the Nile River brought many European explorers seeking fame and fortune. In 1858 British explorer John Hanning Speke traveled to a lake that the Baganda (the Buganda people) called Nnalubale. He named it Lake Victoria, after Britain's Queen Victoria, and claimed that it was the source of the Nile.

Missionaries (religious teachers) came to Buganda to convert the Baganda, who had their own traditional religion, to Christianity. A London-based Protestant group called Church Missionary Society (CMS) sent missionaries to Buganda in 1877. Two years after the CMS established a mission, the first Roman Catholic

FINDING THE NILE

John Hanning Speke was a member of British explorer Richard Burton's 1857–1858 expedition in East Africa following an ancient caravan route. At one point, Burton was too ill to travel farther, so Speke went on a brief trip alone to a nearby lake, which he named Lake Victoria. In his book *The Lake Regions of Central Africa*, Burton described Speke's discovery: "At length my companion had been successful, his 'flying trip' had led him to the northern water, and he had found its dimensions surpassing our most sanguine [bold] expectations. We had scarcely, however, breakfasted, before he announced to me the startling fact that he had discovered the sources of the Nile. It was an inspiration perhaps: the moment he sighted [it] he felt at once no doubt but that the lake at his feet gave birth to that interesting river which has been subject of so much speculation and the object of so many explorers."

missionaries, members of a French order known as the White Fathers, arrived. Protestant, Catholic, and Muslim (Islamic) traders began a fierce religious rivalry to win converts to their own religions. By the mid-1880s, many Baganda had been converted by one of the three groups. Before long, a four-year civil war erupted. After that the victorious Protestant and Catholic converts divided the Buganda kingdom.

Great Britain Gains Control

Great Britain and other Europeans nations wanted to control Africa's natural resources. They needed raw materials, such as minerals and cotton, for their growing industries at home. The British created an empire that included 25 percent of the world's land and people. They struggled with other European nations to gain control over African lands that could supply labor and resources.

> Many nineteenth-century European explorers expected African civilizations to be undeveloped, but many were very sophisticated, with well-organized societies. Frederick Lugard said that the Baganda had achieved "many advances in the scale of humanity which we are wont [used] to accept as indications of [civilization]."

In 1891 Captain Frederick Lugard, a British representative, signed a treaty with Toro. The treaty said that the British would protect Toro from enemy kingdoms and also installed a king of Toro. The king, Kasagama, favored Buganda, which a year earlier had signed a similar treaty with the British.

In 1892 fighting broke out again between Protestant and Catholic converts in Buganda. British and German imperialists (people who want to expand their country's empire) soon entered the conflict. The British sided with the pro-British Protestants, while the Germans sided with the French Catholics. The British eventually won, and Great Britain persuaded Germany to give up its claim to Uganda.

With the Protestant Baganda chiefs as allies, Great Britain sought to take control over the rest of Uganda. It was a slow process. The British government did not want to spend large amounts of money on military campaigns in Uganda, and several kingdoms in Uganda resisted vigorously. Bunyoro-Kitara proved to be the hardest to conquer. By 1894, however, with the help of the Baganda, the British occupied Bunyoro-Kitara. Great Britain established Uganda as a protectorate, or dependent state, on June 18, 1894.

As a reward to the Baganda for their help, the British awarded one-half of Bunyoro-Kitara's conquered territory—territory that became known as the lost counties—to Buganda. In 1900 the British and the Baganda signed the Uganda Agreement, establishing Buganda as a province, or subdivision, within Uganda. The Baganda chiefs would collect taxes throughout the country for the British government. In exchange, Buganda's traditional chiefs kept their local power, though the British had final authority. The agreement also allowed the Baganda chiefs to keep part of Buganda's land. The rest went to the British government—a privilege that other kingdoms did not enjoy, as all their land became British property. Baganda advisers were installed in many of the non-Baganda territories. In 1907 the Banyoro (people of Bunyoro-Kitara) revolted and forced many Baganda chiefs out of Bunyoro, but the counties remained under Buganda's control.

The Toro kingdom also signed a treaty with the British, as did Ankole. The British signed treaties with the people of numerous other, smaller territories and offered rewards to Africans who cooperated with them. But the British used military force to overcome some peoples, especially those in eastern and northeastern Uganda. Superior British weapons overpowered traditional African weapons, including spears, and the Africans' outdated guns. By 1914 the British controlled most of Uganda, which they called the Uganda Protectorate.

The Protectorate Era

The British did not want to settle Ugandan land themselves but used mainly native farmers and workers to reap the resources of the land. In the early years of the British protectorate, Uganda began to reap the benefits of growing cash crops, especially cotton, for the British market. Buganda particularly benefited, as its location on Lake Victoria was ideal for transporting the crop on the new Uganda railroad, built largely by workers from India. (India was also part of the British Empire, like Uganda.) Many of the Indian workers stayed in Uganda, where they became merchants and business owners in the developing country. The railroad stretched from Lake Victoria to the Kenyan city of Mombasa, on the coast of the Indian Ocean.

Great Britain made Uganda a protectorate, rather than a colony. In a protectorate, unlike in a colony, the land rights of native people were recognized. White settlers were not allowed to take land. Great Britain maintained authority and control over the country, however, and exploited the country's resources.

Many Baganda spent their new earnings from crops on imported clothing, bicycles, metal roofing, automobiles,

On **a railroad station platform in Uganda in the early 1900s,** Ugandan workers carry luggage and other bundles of goods for a British traveler *(fourth from left)*.

and, significantly, their children's educations. The Christian missions emphasized learning, and converts quickly learned to read and write in English.

Uganda upgraded its military during World War I (1914–1918). Some Ugandans fought for the British against the Germans in East Africa, though the nation was not largely affected by the war, which mostly took place in Europe and Turkey. A more important issue was the "lost counties" controversy, which revolved around the Bunyoro counties that had been awarded to Buganda in 1894.

In 1921 a group of Banyoro asked the protectorate government to restore the lost counties to Bunyoro. The 1933 Banyoro Agreement established formal relations between the British and the Banyoro, but the sensitive lost counties issue remained unresolved.

During World War II (1939–1945), Uganda upgraded its military once again, and the British protectorate government recruited 77,131 Ugandans to serve in the military on the side of the Allies (Britain and other supporting nations). Ugandans served in present-day Ethiopia, as well as Kenya, Egypt, and the Middle East. Ugandan soldiers returned home from the war with new political and organizational skills.

By then many Ugandans had grown dissatisfied with the British, mostly because they strictly regulated the buying and processing of cash crops. They controlled prices and handed many of the best jobs to Asians, mostly Indians. For example, the British restricted cotton ginning (processing raw cotton)—well-paying work—to Asians only. Indians owned and ran most of the country's industry. Many black Africans, who remained mostly farmers, resented this.

Early Moves toward Independence

After World War II ended in 1945, many Baganda began working for their kingdom to become independent. The Baganda revolted in 1945 and again in 1949, rioting and burning down the houses of pro-government chiefs. The rioters demanded control of the export prices of cotton and an end to the Asian monopoly over cotton ginning. They also demanded to have their own representatives in local government, rather than chiefs appointed by the British. They were critical as well of the young kabaka, Frederick Walugembe Mutesa II (also known as Kabaka Freddie), whom they said ignored the needs of his people.

These incidents of revolt alarmed the British and other Ugandans, who opposed a separate Buganda. A Uganda without its most populous and wealthiest province would suffer economically. It might also encourage other groups to fight for separate independence. The British were preparing instead for an independent—and united—nation of Uganda. Weakened by World War II, they had already begun dismantling other parts of their empire, pulling out of other African nations and India.

In January 1952, Andrew Cohen became the governor of Uganda. Cohen felt strongly that Buganda should remain a province within a united, independent Uganda. He made a series of economic and political changes to achieve his goals. For example, he helped get cotton-ginning jobs for Africans and set fair prices for African-grown coffee. He also reorganized the lawmaking branch of government so it included African representatives.

The Kabaka Crisis

Cohen's reforms alarmed many Baganda politicians, who saw that power would be shifting away from them to the national level, which Bagandans feared would be dominated by white settlers' interests. In 1953 Cohen met with Kabaka Freddie to discuss this and other issues. But Kabaka Freddie refused to cooperate, demanding that Buganda be separated from the rest of the protectorate. Cohen had him deported to Great Britain.

Though Kabaka Freddie had been unpopular with his subjects, he was a symbol of their culture. His deportation turned him into a hero. Baganda of all parts of society demanded that their leader be returned. Two years later, he was.

A new Uganda Agreement required Buganda to abandon demands for a separate independence. But the majority of the agreement was a great victory for the Baganda. For the first time since 1889, the kabaka held the power to appoint and dismiss his chiefs. Previously he had been only a figurehead. He became a leader in deciding how Uganda would be governed. The agreement also strengthened Buganda's position in Uganda. The deportation and return of Kabaka Freddie, called the kabaka crisis, led to considerable tension between Buganda and the other kingdoms in the protectorate.

Independence Is Gained

As these tensions between Buganda and those opposed to its domination increased, national political parties began to emerge. One of the first was the Progressive Party (PP), a Protestant Baganda party, formed in 1955. The next year, Roman Catholic Baganda formed their own party, the Democratic Party (DP). Outside Buganda, political organizer Milton Obote formed a new party, the Uganda

Sir Andrew Cohen, the British governor of Uganda *(left, front)*, and **Kabaka Freddie** Mutasa II *(second from right, front)* attend the signing of an agreement that allowed Kabaka Freddie to return to Uganda and granted him additional powers.

People's Congress (UPC), in 1960. The UPC drew most of its support from the Protestant population outside Buganda, as well as some Muslims.

In preparation for independence, the British government organized national elections in Uganda in March 1961, but separatist Baganda boycotted them. As a result, the DP won the elections and a DP member was appointed chief minister. This alarmed the British, who were largely Protestant and worried about Catholic control. It also alarmed the separatist Baganda, who had second thoughts about the wisdom of their election boycott. These separatists formed a political party called Kabaka Yekka (KY), or the King Only.

The British arranged another election before independence, to which the KY quickly agreed. Prior to the election, the KY and UPC joined to defeat the DP. As a result, a new government made up of this UPC-KY coalition was elected. Obote, as prime minister, and Mutesa II, as president, led Uganda when it gained its formal independence on October 9, 1962.

◉ Early Independence

The UPC-KY coalition was a fragile partnership. After several years of political differences among different factions (groups), unity within the UPC began to crumble. To solidify his power, in 1966 Obote promoted a loyal junior officer, Idi Amin, to army chief. He then suspended the 1962 constitution and forced a new constitution through parliament (the lawmaking body). The constitution abolished the powers the kingdoms had in federal government, reduced the power of Uganda's traditional leaders, and stripped the presidency from the kabaka. It put presidential powers into the hands of the prime minister—Obote.

Buganda rejected the new constitution and ordered the central government to leave the kingdom's soil. In response, Obote sent troops led by Amin to the kabaka's palace. Although Kabaka Mutesa II climbed a palace wall and fled the country to London, the incident resulted in more than one hundred deaths and crushed any open opposition to Obote.

In 1967 Obote introduced another constitution. This one abolished Uganda's four kingdoms altogether and gave him even more power.

Obote retained power by relying on Idi Amin and the army, but relations with Amin were growing weaker. After the murder of Amin's sole rival among senior army officers early in 1970—which some government officials believed was arranged by Amin—

Obote's wariness of Amin grew. Finally, in January 1971, Obote ordered Amin and his supporters to be arrested. Obote then left the country. News of the order was leaked to Amin, who responded on January 25 by staging a coup, or sudden overthrow of the government. He sent his loyal troops into Kampala and the airport in Entebbe and easily defeated Obote's disorganized troops.

Idi Amin

Amin declared himself president, but he ruled as a dictator. He dissolved the parliament and changed the constitution to give himself total power. During the first year of his dictatorship, he ordered mass executions of troops he believed to be pro-Obote, especially troops of Acholi and Langi ethnicity.

Amin's government was run by military commanders and military tribunals (courts), with soldiers holding top government posts. Amin allowed government agents to commit brutal acts, and people lost confidence in government. He spent much of his time enlarging and controlling the army. The military became a source of problems, as different groups fought among themselves and violent revenge grew common. Paying for the military was also a constant concern, and Amin spent money on the army instead of social services.

Uganda's relationships with Great Britain and another chief ally, the Jewish state of Israel, deteriorated quickly. (Israel, when it was called Palestine, had been part of the British Empire.) Amin converted to Islam and forged an alliance with the Muslim nation of Libya, an enemy of Israel, which provided financial and military aid. In March 1972, Amin broke off diplomatic relations with Israel and ordered all Israelis out of the country. Uganda also forged alliances with Saudi Arabia and the Soviet Union (a union of fifteen republics, including Russia). Both provided aid to Uganda.

Amin also expelled nearly all of the fifty thousand Asians, mostly Indians, from Uganda. They had controlled much of the country's commerce and owned many businesses. Amin took these businesses without paying for them, thus destroying economic order. People who could fled, and the country lost many of its educated workers and businesspeople. Social services such as health care and education broke down. Illegal economic networks brought great wealth to a small number of people, but many people had to turn to subsistence farming (growing only enough to feed their families) for survival. In addition, thousands of people Amin saw as enemies were jailed, murdered, or simply disappeared. General terror and insecurity became a way of life for Ugandans.

By 1978 Amin's hold on power had become uncertain. Troops that had once been reliable rebelled. In October Amin sent troops still loyal to him against the rebels, some of whom fled to Tanzania. Amin then accused Tanzania of waging war against Uganda, and he invaded Tanzanian territory.

Tanzania, joined by Ugandans opposed to Amin united as the Uganda National Liberation Army (UNLA), counterattacked. Tanzania and the UNLA took Kampala in April 1979. Idi

BIG DADDY

Idi Amin, who liked to be called Big Daddy, became internationally well known for his unusual behavior. When he became president of Uganda, for instance, he declared himself "the last king of Scotland" and had his personal guard play Scottish bagpipes and wear Scottish kilts (skirts worn by men). He had been a soldier in a Scottish regiment in East Africa when he was a young man and had admired the Scots for their independent attitude toward the English. He also took the title, "His Excellency President for Life Field Marshal Al Hadj Doctor Idi Amin Dada, VC, DSO, MC, Lord of All the Beasts of the Earth and Fishes of the Sea and Conqueror of the British Empire in Africa in General and Uganda in Particular." While he sometimes seemed comical, his public brutality was not comical. Once he ordered the beheading of political prisoners to be shown on television and ordered the victims to wear white so their blood could easily be seen.

President Idi Amin delivers a speech after a parade in Koboko, Uganda, in January 1978.

Tanzanian soldiers aided Ugandan rebels fighting to end Amin's rule. In April 1979, they burned factories in Kampala.

Amin fled by air, first to Libya and later to Saudi Arabia. He left behind a society that had almost totally fallen apart.

Interim Government and Obote's Second Reign

After Amin left, several short-lived governments tried to maintain order and establish a unified Ugandan government. In May 1980, Paulo Muwanga, Obote's right-hand man, carried out a bloodless (nonviolent) coup. Shortly afterward, Obote returned from Tanzania and began to rally his former UPC supporters.

In December 1980, Uganda held elections for the first time in eighteen years. The main parties running were the DP and the UPC. Though the UPC employed intimidation tactics to influence the vote, the DP won 81 of 126 seats in parliament. But Muwanga seized control of the Electoral Commission, which had the power to count the ballots. He then announced a UPC victory, with 72 seats. Obote again became prime minister.

Shortly after Obote's second government took office in February 1981, several rival groups began to challenge it. One of the most important groups was formed by Yoweri Museveni, a former Military Commission member, and his armed supporters. They called themselves the National Resistance Army (NRA). Obote fought these rivals with his Uganda National Liberation Army, made up primarily of Acholi and Langi soldiers. Most of them had little training or discipline. Once again, as during the Amin regime, the military and police abducted and detained citizens, and many people simply disappeared.

The army began to split along ethnic lines. Acholi soldiers complained that they were given too much frontline action and too few rewards for their services. Obote then appointed a Langi as general, further angering Acholi soldiers. As he did in January 1971, Obote left the capital after giving orders for the arrest of a leading Acholi commander, Basilio Okello. Okello then mobilized troops and entered Kampala on July 27, 1985.

Obote fled the country for Zambia, allegedly taking much of the national treasury with him. The overall death toll during his reign from 1981 to 1985 was estimated to be as high as 500,000.

President Museveni

Okello established the Military Council to govern the country until elections could be held later in the year. In August, however, Museveni's NRA began a military campaign to overthrow Okello, and in a couple months, it controlled large parts of the country. In January 1986, the NRA took Kampala, forcing Okello to flee the country, and dissolved the Military Council. Museveni and his followers created a political group called the National Resistance Movement (NRM), known as the Movement. All other political groups and activity were banned, as the government sought to establish order. Museveni was sworn in as president, the head of the government. The National Resistance Council (NRC), made up of presidential appointees, was formed to legislate. President Museveni pledged to end his interim government within four years in favor of an elected government with a new constitution. Museveni's government reinstated the four kingdoms—abolished by Obote—including the kabakaship as a ceremonial office only.

Yoweri Museveni *(far right)* was forty-two years old when he began to rule Uganda in 1986.

Defeated rebel forces and guerrilla (nontraditional fighter) groups remained active in Uganda, and several groups sought to overthrow the new government. One opposition group, the Holy Spirit movement, rose in rebellion in northern and eastern Uganda. By late 1987, the rebellion was suppressed, with about five thousand Holy Spirit rebels killed. Surviving members regrouped and formed the antigovernment Lord's Resistance Army (LRA).

In 1989 the NRC extended the interim period of government for six more years, considering the country still unstable. In 1991 the NRA made a campaign through the north and east to combat rebel activity, killing at least fifteen hundred guerrillas and arresting more than one thousand.

Fighting between the army and the LRA ruined the economy in the northern and western parts of Uganda. The LRA killed as many as ten thousand people between 1993 and 1998. Devastatingly, by 1999 the LRA had also kidnapped about ten thousand children to use as soldiers and slaves.

Attacks by the LRA, who had established bases in southern Sudan, continued. In 2002 Sudan allowed Ugandan troops to pursue the LRA into Sudan, and all four main LRA bases in Sudan were captured. However, LRA activity surged again in 2003. The LRA survives by raiding villages and camps of Ugandans displaced by rebel activity, stealing food and provisions, mutilating and killing people, and continuing to abduct young people.

The LRA has abducted more than 20,000 children and caused the displacement of about 1.5 million people during eighteen years of fighting.

Terrorism and opposition to the government continued to threaten stability in Uganda, as did tensions with troubled neighboring countries. Museveni has had an aggressive foreign policy with Rwanda and especially Congo, where Uganda intervened in a civil war in 1998. Uganda withdrew troops from Congo in 2003, but conflict there continues to rage. Years of civil war and ethnic violence in Sudan have driven refugees across the border into Uganda. Also, tensions over the status of Buganda remain. In January 2003, about 200,000 Baganda demonstrated in Kampala for a new federal constitution and semiautonomous status for their kingdom.

All the same, Museveni has had successes. Under his leadership, Uganda steadily moved away from the violence of past regimes (although his government has a record of human rights violations) and toward a stable government. In some parts of the country, ethnic tensions have declined noticeably. He invited Asians back, and many have returned.

His government launched a largely successful attack on AIDS and encouraged the empowerment of women, with almost 25 percent of parliamentary seats reserved for women. Uganda's vice president, Specioza Wandira Kazibwe (serving from 1994 to 2003), was the first woman vice president in Africa. And Museveni has obtained considerable foreign aid to help his country, which is desperately poor and faces challenges in all areas.

In 2004 the LRA and the government held face-to-face peace talks for the first time. No solution was reached.

In 2005 the nation votes on whether the constitution should be changed, which would allow Museveni to run for a third term as president in the 2006 elections. The referendum (vote) will also ask citizens if they want to change the constitution to allow a multiparty system. In the past, Museveni's "no-party" system was seen as more stable because political parties based on ethnic and religious groups had previously divided the country. It is hoped that reintroducing multiple parties will allow for more open political debate and a stronger democratic system.

Look for links to election results and other current events in Uganda at www.vgsbooks.com.

Government

Uganda is a republic—citizens elect their leaders—and it is governed according to law. After years of Museveni's interim NRM government, Uganda adopted a new constitution in 1995. It established the office of executive president, who is elected by the people every five years. The president is both chief of state and head of government. The Constitution limits the president to two terms.

The parliament, called the National Assembly, is the legislative, or lawmaking, branch of the government. Members serve five-year terms. The 214 parliamentary members are elected directly by voters. The president nominates 76 members to guarantee representation of all members of society: 56 women, 5 youth, 5 disabled, and 10 army members. The head of the parliament is called the prime minister and is appointed by the president. Members of parliament serve five-year terms.

The legal system is based on English and traditional law. The Supreme Court heads the judicial branch of government. Magistrate's courts, high courts, and courts of appeals operate under the Supreme Court.

The country is divided into fifty-six administrative districts. These are divided into counties and villages. Elected officials function at each level. All adults of eighteen years or older have the right to vote.

THE PEOPLE

In the early twenty-first century, Uganda's population was 26.1 million people. Compared to other African nations south of the Sahara Desert, Uganda is a densely populated country with about 271 people per square mile (105 people per square km). Sub-Saharan Africa as a whole has only about 76 people per square mile (29 per sq. km). Uganda is growing at a 3 percent rate of natural increase and is projected to have about 47 million people by 2025 and 82 million by 2050. About 51 percent of the population is under the age of fifteen. Only about 2 percent of Ugandans are older than sixty-five. Although the majority of Ugandans live in the south, where most cities are, only about 12 percent of the people live in urban centers. That portion is growing steadily, but it is still less than half the rate for sub-Saharan Africa in general, where 30 percent of people live in cities. Most Ugandans work as farmers. They live in family homesteads surrounded by their gardens and fields. Others make a living by herding cattle. They live in groups and move with their herds, in search of pasture and water.

Ethnic Groups

With dozens of ethnic groups, Ugandan society is diverse. Most ethnic groups have their own language, and ethnic groups are usually described by the language they speak. The population can be divided into four major language groups, Bantu, Nilotic, Nilo-Hamitic, and Sudanic. Generally, those in the south speak Bantu languages and those in the central part of the north speak Nilotic languages. Those in the northeast speak Nilo-Hamitic languages, and those in the northwest speak Sudanic languages (developed in central and western Africa). Each language group in turn has many subgroups, each with different, complex social backgrounds. This diversity has historically caused great divisions among Uganda's people and tended to destabilize the nation, as different ethnic groups have competed for political, economic, and military advantage.

Bantu speakers make up 89 percent of the nation's population. Among the Bantu speakers are the Bugosa, Bagisu, and the Baganda.

The Baganda are the country's largest ethnic group. They speak a type of Bantu called Luganda.

A little more than 10 percent of the population are Nilotic speakers (the next largest group after Bantu speakers). Several groups of people speak Nilotic languages: the Lango people live in the north, near Lake Kyoga. The Acholi also live in the north, near the conflict-ridden Sudanese border. The Iteso and Karamajong live in the east and are related to the Maasai people of Kenya.

Uganda is also host to several nonindigenous groups, though non-Africans make up only 1 percent of the population. Europeans, Asians—especially Indians—and Arabs have settled in Uganda. About 50,000 Indians fled the country when Idi Amin expelled them in 1972. President Museveni has welcomed Indians to Uganda again, and a few thousand have returned. Some have had property and possessions returned to them. Uganda is also home to about 500,000 refugees from several neighboring countries, as well as internally displaced persons (IDPs), who number about 1.6 million in northern Uganda. It is believed that more than 200,000 Sudanese fled to Uganda in 2004.

Women

Ugandan women have historically been considered subordinate, or socially inferior, to men and were expected to show their subordination publicly, for instance by kneeling to men. In most parts of Uganda, women could not own land or grow crops for their own profit. Women usually did most of the child care and farming. Men often married more than one woman, an illegal practice. Women who were divorced or widowed had no rights to their husband's property or their own children. But women had some traditional rights that gave them influence and power. Women could be important religious leaders. Multiple wives sometimes worked together to share power and gain influence.

During the 1960s, the Uganda Council of Women worked to obtain rights for women to own property and keep custody of their children if their marriages ended. The council also worked to have marriage, divorce, and inheritance laws written and publicized to ensure fair treatment in these areas. In 1976 the Uganda Association of Women Lawyers was founded, and in 1988 the association created a legal aid clinic to help women facing the loss of property or children due to divorce, separation, or the death of their husband. It also sought to expand educational opportunities—including legal education—for women and to assist women and children who were victims of AIDS. In 2003 Specioza Wandira Kazibwe, Uganda's vice president from 1994 to 2003, broke a taboo against speaking publicly about home life when she divorced her husband of twenty years, revealing that he had physically abused her for years. This helped raise awareness of domestic violence, a major challenge for many Ugandan women.

Years of violent conflict in Uganda left many women widowed or deserted and forced to rely on themselves to support their families. The Museveni government has tried to end discrimination against women, and many women are active in politics. Uganda's constitution, adopted in 1995, requires that women make up almost 25 percent of the parliament.

This **Ugandan woman** holding a child is wearing a *busuti*, the traditional Ugandan blouse and skirt. Their style varies from one ethnic group to another. The Museveni government has worked to improve the lives of the women and children in Uganda.

MARRIAGE AND MOTHERHOOD

Most boys and girls in Uganda marry when they are still in their teens. About 47 percent of females between the ages of fifteen and nineteen are married. Marrying for love is common, but a couple's parents must approve the marriage. When a young man wants to marry a young woman, he gives her parents a "bridewealth," a set of gifts that might include cattle, goats, and chickens, as well as Western clothing or televisions. A husband may reclaim the gifts if his wife does not become pregnant. About 66 percent of Ugandan women have given birth by the age of twenty, and a woman has an average of 7 children in her lifetime. About 30 percent of Ugandan men have more than one wife although it is officially illegal.

Extended Family

Though Ugandans come from many different backgrounds with different lifestyles—and though their culture has been greatly influenced by British control—certain characteristics of Ugandan society are shared by all. Almost all Ugandans place great importance on the extended family such as grandparents, aunts and uncles, and cousins. Tradition requires that Ugandans be responsible not only for immediate family but also for extended family, including distant relations. Family members in need must be welcomed and helped when they have hard times. Ugandans share their wealth and joy as well as their sorrows and struggles. For example, if a person has a poor harvest and needs food, he or she can depend on extended family to help.

This responsibility can be overwhelming, especially in times when war or conflict or AIDS has torn families apart. Taking care of the basic needs of so many people can leave a person little or no money, and as a result, many young Ugandans have left their villages to seek jobs in the cities. Some of these people still share their fortunes with their families, but others have avoided or been unable to meet their family duties altogether.

Health

In spite of nearly constant warfare and other violence, poor medical facilities, disease, and poverty, Uganda's total population has grown steadily and quickly since independence in 1962, from about 7 million to more than 26 million. During British rule, the introduction of Western medicine (especially preventive medicine that protects against infectious diseases) has played an important role in this growth. Relocation of large numbers of people away from tsetse-fly-infested areas to protect them from sleeping sickness spread by the flies is a good example. Uganda faces many dangerous diseases, including measles, respiratory tract infections, diarrhea, tetanus, malaria, tuberculosis, whooping cough, and AIDS.

The British established an effective medical system when Uganda was under British rule, but Idi Amin and his soldiers destroyed this system. Under Amin's rule, doctors, nurses, and other medical personnel fled the country, and fighting destroyed many hospitals and clinics. Later leaders did little to undo the damage, but the current government has rebuilt many hospitals and clinics. The infant mortality rate is about 88 deaths for every 1,000 live births, slightly better than the average for sub-Saharan Africa as a whole, which is 93 for every thousand live births. Only about one hospital bed is available for every 1,000 people in Uganda. Life expectancy is only about 44 years (43 for men, 46 for women). The death rate is about 17 deaths per year per 1,000 people. An average of 124 out of every 1,000 children die before the age of five. Clean water is available to

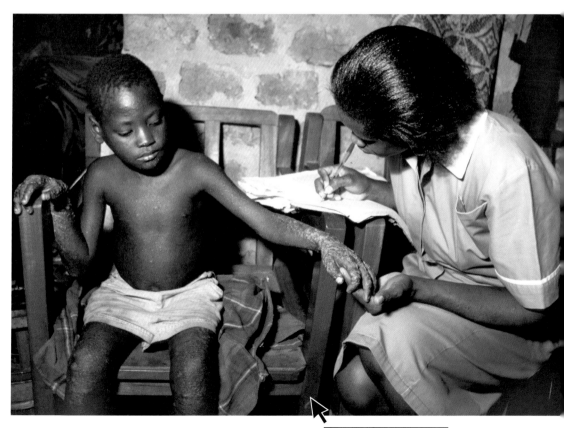

In Kampala, Uganda, a nurse checks to see how a young AIDS patient is doing. He is lucky to live in an urban area where a nurse can visit his home.

80 percent of the people, and 75 percent have access to sanitation (running water, indoor plumbing, and garbage disposal).

AIDS is Uganda's biggest health challenge. By the early 1990s, about 30 percent of adult Ugandans (aged 15 to 49) were infected. In Uganda the disease is nicknamed "slim" because it makes victims lose so much weight. About 55 percent of adult AIDS victims are women, which has resulted in many children being infected through their mothers, either before birth or through breastfeeding. There is no cure for AIDS and no vaccine for HIV (human immunodeficiency virus, which sometimes causes AIDS). The drugs that help HIV/AIDS victims are too expensive for the average Ugandan. The best defense is prevention.

President Museveni has encouraged citizens to talk freely about AIDS, putting aside cultural taboos against talking about sex. Public service advertisements and radio reminders about safe sex push a national "ABC" plan: Abstinence (abstain from sex), Be faithful (have only one sexual partner), and use Condoms (to help prevent passage of HIV during sex). In 1986, along with the World Health Organization (WHO), the government created an organization to focus on AIDS education, safe blood supply (HIV, the virus that causes AIDS is transmitted through blood or body fluids), monitoring the epidemic, and patient care. Uganda has also established AIDS clinics all over the country, with testing and counseling available. In 1992 the Uganda AIDS Commission was created to control the spread of HIV. In spite of these positive steps, AIDS has caused tens of thousands of deaths (84,000 by 2001) in Uganda as well as hundreds of thousands of orphans whose parents have died of AIDS in the twenty-first century. Many of these children have to raise themselves and their siblings.

President Museveni used an old proverb (traditional saying) to describe the need for AIDS education in Uganda: "When a lion comes into your village, you must raise the alarm loudly."

Uganda has been one of the most successful African nations in the fight against AIDS through its bold and strong prevention program. As a result of this program, the rate of infection in the early twenty-first century was down to about 5 percent. Though 5 percent is epidemic (affecting a disproportionately large number of individuals in the country), it is better than the rate for sub-Saharan Africa as a whole, in which 8.9 percent of adults are infected.

Another health risk that has been reduced is female genital mutilation (FGM), the partial or

A group of girls in Masaka, Uganda, dance and sing a song about preventing AIDS.

total removal of the female external genitalia. FGM is a long-standing tradition, usually as an initiation rite, that is entrenched in the lives of many East African women. Cultural beliefs help keep FGM in practice, despite a variety of serious health risks, including deadly infections. In recent years, FGM has been discouraged in East Africa. As with the battle against AIDS, Uganda is in the forefront of this battle, and FGM has been outlawed in Uganda. About 5 percent of females in Uganda have undergone FGM, compared to between 10 and 18 percent in Tanzania. Even in northeastern Uganda, the only part of the country where FGM is still commonly practiced, support is decreasing.

Education

Traditional education in Uganda concentrated on teaching oral traditions and survival skills. It also created a sense of fellowship and community among students. Later, Muslim and Christian educators stressed their religions as well as the importance of literacy (the ability to read and write). Europeans also taught subjects such as science, arithmetic, and history, as well as agricultural skills. Western education offered the best chance for students to improve their lives, and as a result, increasing numbers of Ugandans attended European schools.

Modern Uganda has a formal education system, and the nation's school system is well developed. It has about eight thousand elementary schools, eight hundred secondary (junior high and high) schools, ninety-four primary teacher training colleges, and fifty other postsecondary institutions, chief among them being Makerere University in Kampala. A university of science and technology is located at Mbarara and a small Islamic university is at Mbale.

Education is not compulsory, but about 89 percent of eligible children attend a public or private primary school. The government pays for up to four children per family to attend primary school. Primary school attendance has doubled since Museveni became president in 1986. The government is striving to achieve 100 percent primary school attendance. In several districts, however, especially where refugees have settled and where the LRA has spread terror, high attendance rates are more difficult to achieve. One strategy the government and other nongovernment organizations have been working on is mobile schools, which can move with people who are forced to move or flee.

> "People are not going to school in the war ravaged areas, the young are being wasted away, those who are lucky enough to survive are being swallowed up in diseases erupting from the congestion and poor living conditions, those who will survive to the end will be lucky if they come out half sane, so what good are we the Acholi as a tribe then?"
>
> —Monica Arac de Nyeko, "Northern Uganda . . . No Hope?" *Sunday Monitor*, 2002

The government also hopes to get better attendance and standardized test scores from children who work herding cattle, farming, or otherwise have difficulty regularly attending school. Thousands of students have been enrolled in alternative schools, where hours are flexible. This allows students to study and help with work at home, such as fishing and making fishing nets or looking after cows. Studies in these alternative schools are often tailored to such students. In herding communities, a child's arithmetic education may begin with cows—counting and adding a cow's legs, for example.

Another challenge for the education program is to improve the ratio of teachers to students.

Secondary schools in Uganda traditionally charge fees. Only 9 percent of females and 15 percent of males attend secondary school, partly due to a shortage of secondary schools and secondary school teachers. Roughly 70 percent of the adult population of Uganda is literate, including 79 percent of males and 60 percent of females.

Visit www.vgsbooks.com for links to websites with additional information about the people of Uganda.

CULTURAL LIFE

Ugandans are proud of their heritage. Besides maintaining traditional ways, indigenous culture often blends with modern Western culture. The traditional culture is rich in song, dance, and drama, while Western technology such as video cameras are eagerly sought after. Most Ugandans value religion and spirituality, and the majority of people are Christian or Muslim. However, traditional religions remain, and syncretism, the blending of traditional religions with Christianity or Islam is common too. Folk art blends function with beauty, and everyday objects such as baskets and pottery are aesthetic as well as useful objects. Ugandans are very friendly and enjoy gathering to eat meals together, to play traditional games, such as the board game mweso, or to socialize at a soccer game.

◉ Religion and Holidays

Throughout Uganda's history, religion has played an important role in people's lives. About two-thirds of Ugandans are Christian, with

33 percent being Roman Catholic and 33 percent being Protestant. Another 16 percent are Muslims, practitioners of Islam, while 18 percent hold to traditional religions or do not practice any religion. The small number of Indians who returned to the country under Museveni's government practice the Hindu or Sikh religions.

Traditional religions are most common in rural areas. In traditional religions, priests take care of both the physical and spiritual well-being of their communities. They give medical advice, moral and social guidance, and maintain a positive relationship between the community and its god or gods. All but one of Uganda's ethnic groups believe in one supreme being. The exception is the Baganda traditionalists, who believe in several gods. Several groups, including the Baganda, also worship real and mythical ancestors. Such groups believe that the dead know what their living family members are doing and care about them. They regard the living as their children. Families appease their ancestors through sacrifices and honor them during festivals.

BAGANDA RELIGION

In the Baganda belief system, people worship many gods, and most spiritual beings are considered to be the source of bad fortune, such as hunger and bad weather. The purpose of many Baganda rituals is to keep these beings satisfied.

The Baganda religion also serves to strengthen the role of the kabaka. Though the kabaka is not considered to be descended from gods, his skill as a leader is judged in part by how well he defends his people from punishment at the hands of angry gods.

Important gods in the Baganda religion include Mukasa, the god of children and fertility; Kibuka and Nende, the gods of war; Nagawoni, the goddess of hunger; a number of gods of the elements, including rain, lightning, earthquakes, and drought; gods of the diseases plague and smallpox; and a god of hunting. These gods are kept content through sacrifices, including sacrifices of food, animals, and, at times in the past, human beings.

They tell their stories through song, music, and dance. When a person dies, the family may perform rituals to ensure the person's safe arrival in the next world, the world of the family's ancestors.

The majority of Muslims live in southern Uganda. Islam arose on the Arabian Peninsula in the seventh century A.D. The Prophet Muhammad was its founder. Muslims believe that Muhammad received a series of revelations, written down as the Quran, the holy book of Islam. The religion was brought to Uganda when Arab and Swahili (Muslim Africans from the Indian Ocean coast) slave and ivory traders reached the country in the mid-nineteenth century. Muslim soldiers also brought Islam from Sudan.

Christianity (both Catholicism and Protestantism) was introduced by European missionaries in the late nineteenth century and came to be the dominant religion in Uganda. Tensions between Protestants and Catholics have at times been high, and President Museveni has tried to ease these tensions by refusing to be identified with either group.

The Abayudaya of Uganda are a small community of approximately six hundred Jewish citizens. They live in eastern Uganda near Mbale.

Many of Uganda's public holidays are religious. Muslim holidays include the holy month of Ramadan, the ninth month of the Muslim calendar, when practicing Muslims take no food and drink from sunrise to sunset; Eid al-Fitr, a time of feasting that marks the end of Ramadan; and Eid al-Adha, the Feast of the Sacrifice, celebrated in February. Christian holidays include Easter in the spring, Christmas on December 25, and Martyrs' Day on June 3. Martyrs' Day

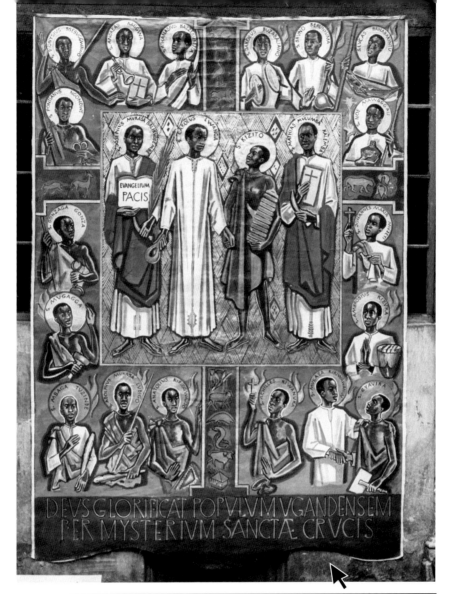

Dozens of **Ugandan Christians were tortured and killed near Kampala, Uganda,** between 1885 and 1887. Pope Paul VI canonized twenty-two of them (made them saints) on October 18, 1964, in Rome, Italy. These saints are represented on the banner above. In modern times, they are known as the martyrs of Uganda.

is when Christian Ugandans remember Christians in the late 1800s who were willing to be martyred (die for their religious faith) rather than to renounce Christianity as the kabaka had ordered them to do. The Abayudaya observe traditional Jewish holidays. Secular (nonreligious) holidays include New Year's Day, Liberation Day (January 26, when the NRM came to power), International Women's Day (March 8), Labor Day (May 1), National Heroes' Day (June 9), Independence Day (October 9), and Boxing Day (December 26). Community festivals mark the cycles of life, such as weddings and births and the growing season. Festivals celebrate the first rain of the season, planting, and harvesting crops. They are cause for music and dancing, eating and drinking.

One of the largest independent radio stations in Uganda is Simba. You can get a link to a site where you can listen to it, and also to Radio Uganda, at www.vgsbooks.com.

The Media and the Arts

Since President Museveni came to power, there have been considerable changes in both the print and electronic media. State-owned Uganda Radio broadcasts throughout the country in English and several other languages. The government loosened its control of the media in 1993, and since then many independent radio and television stations have been established. The government has at times criticized some of the almost one hundred private radio and television stations, accusing some of raising ethnic tension.

The most important daily newspaper is *New Vision*. Although it is state owned, it has a lot of independence and often publishes articles critical of the government. The other major daily is the *Monitor*, an independent newspaper.

Visual arts are important in Ugandan life. Makerere University has established the Margaret Trowell School of Fine Art, whose graduates find jobs as graphic artists, art teachers, and artists. Museums and art galleries in Uganda display collections of paintings, local crafts, and musical instruments. Pottery of assorted sizes and designs is particularly popular. Some pieces of pottery seen in Uganda have been created over the centuries of Uganda's history, and others have been created in contemporary times. Some artists use bark cloth as a canvas for paintings. Other art forms include woodcarving, decorated gourds, woven baskets, weapons, and musical instruments.

Music and dancing play a prominent role in Ugandan culture, particularly in traditional life. They often reflect the way of life of the people who perform them. Drums, xylophones (wooden bars struck with mallets), lyres (small stringed harps), and thumb pianos (metal strips mounted on wood or a gourd, plucked with fingers) are the main musical instruments. The music of herding people generally has cattle as a theme, and sometimes their dances imitate the movements of cattle. Agricultural people tend to emphasize farming activities in their songs and dances. Hunters and people who traditionally lived in forest areas mimic the sounds of birds and other animals in their music. Their dancing costumes may be skins of animals. Music and dance also play a role in religious rituals.

Modern Ugandans also enjoy popular music, such as hip-hop, gospel, and reggae, and going to dance clubs. Perhaps Uganda's most popular musical group is the Afrigo Band, who combine rumba and pop. The band has produced seventeen albums since it was founded in 1976. The band writes and sings primarily in local Ugandan languages, though in recent times, it has recorded in English, Swahili, and French in an attempt to gain worldwide popularity. Moses Matovu is the reed player, vocalist, and leader of the Afrigo Band.

The Roman Catholic Lubaga Cathedral in Kampala is the home base of a hip-hop gospel group of five Ugandan youths. They began performing together in 1999 and call themselves THE WOGS (Take Him Everywhere, Witnesses of God's Salvation).

The female artist Titi was voted best female artist at the first Pearl of Africa Music (PAM) Awards in 2003. The awards were created to recognize Ugandan musicians and to help raise the quality of music in Uganda to international standards. In 2004 Titi released a hit song called "Nsonyiwa Faza," about a married woman who has taken a new lover. Though men sometimes have more than one wife, the song has caused a stir in Uganda, a conservative society where it is hard for many to imagine a married woman having feelings for another man.

Musicians play a xylophone in Kasese, a small town situated near Queen Elizabeth National Park at the base of the Ruwenzori Mountains. It is the last place for hikers to buy supplies before entering the park.

Also important are the performance arts, centered on the National Theatre in Kampala, the venue for annual music and drama festivals and the headquarters for the Uganda Theatrical Groups Association. Uganda has also developed a small film industry.

Language and Literature

Counts vary on how many languages are spoken in Uganda, though there are probably close to forty. English is the official language and is used in government, business, schools, and the media, though less than 30 percent of Ugandans understand English. Most who do live in urban areas. Uganda has no one language that is understood by everyone. English, Swahili, and Luganda are the most commonly spoken. In rural areas, people generally speak an indigenous language, and many know a second language—often a European language. Less than 1 percent speak Arabic, the main language of the Middle East.

Swahili, a Bantu language, comes from the Swahili people, Muslims who live on the east coast of Africa. Swahili is the official language of Kenya and Tanzania, the other East African nations. During the 1970s, Idi Amin tried to encourage national unity by extending the use of Swahili. In modern times, many Ugandans have argued that Uganda should adopt Swahili as a second official language. They claim that this would help unify Uganda, something many believe the nation desperately needs. Opponents of making Swahili an official language maintain that English is the language of international commerce and politics. They feel that using English would help Ugandans develop their country.

Ugandans did not have a written language before the British arrived. People passed along tales about their ancestors, myths, and history through stories and songs. After colonization, which brought formal education, much oral literature was written down. Books from Western culture were introduced to Uganda during the protectorate period as well. Still, oral literature remains a valuable part of Ugandan life. In societies that maintain oral rather than written literature, people develop strong memory skills.

Ugandans also began to produce their own written literature during the protectorate period. Sir Apolo Kagwa, prime minister of Uganda from 1899 to 1926, was a well-known author in Uganda. Kagwa wrote several books about the history and customs of the Baganda and other peoples. Okot p'Bitek (1931–1982) wrote several books, including the novel *Lak Tar (White Teeth)* (1953), and a series of poetic stories, including *Song of Lawino* (1969) and *Song of Ocal* (1970).

An elder tells young people a traditional folktale in Kampala, Uganda. Read a lively folktale from Uganda yourself, and learn more about Uganda's traditional and modern culture by visiting www.vgsbooks.com for links.

An important contemporary Ugandan author is Yasmin Alibhai-Brown, whose work has become well known in Great Britain. Alibhai-Brown graduated from Kampala's Makerere University in 1972 and then left Uganda for Great Britain. She has written for many international publications, such as the *New York Times* and *Newsweek*. She published her autobiography, *No Place Like Home*, in 1995. Alibhai-Brown has won many awards for her journalism and books.

Women writers, many of whom write in English, have organized a group, the Ugandan Women's Writers Association, known as Femrite. Monica Arac de Nyeko is a member of Femrite and a fiction writer and journalist. In 2002 she completed her first novel for young adults, *Out of Ebony*. Margaret Snyder has written several books about the Ugandan women's movement. She is a founding director of the United Nations Development Fund for Women (UNIFEM). Barbara Kimenye is a Ugandan children's author who has found popularity all over East Africa. A selection of women authors can be found in the book *A Woman's Voice: An Anthology of Short Stories by Ugandan Women*, edited by Mary Karooro Okurut.

Ugandan writer Moses Isegawa published his first novel, *Abyssinian Chronicles,* in 2000 to great reviews. It is the story of a young man growing up in Uganda during the violent 1970s and 1980s. A second novel, *Snakepit,* was published in spring 2004 to similar critical praise. This book is set within Idi Amin's corrupt government. Another successful contemporary Ugandan writer is Mahmood Mamdani, one of Africa's best-known intellectuals. He has written several books, including *When Victims Become Killers*

Moses Isegawa

(2002), an examination of the mass killings in neighboring Rwanda in the 1990s. In 2004 Mamdani published *Good Muslim, Bad Muslim,* a discussion of modern-day terrorism. Other important Ugandan writers include Ham Mukasa, Daudi Chwa II, E. S. Kironde, and William Kigongo.

Clothing

Ugandans commonly wear a combination of traditional and modern dress. For daily occasions, most Ugandan men wear Western-style

Bark cloth has had several uses in the many traditional cultures of Uganda. Artists have painted on it. Writers have written on it. People have worn it, although less frequently since Arab traders brought cotton cloth to Uganda in the late 1800s. Bark cloth is made by peeling sheets of bark from fig trees and soaking the sheets until they are soft and the outer bark comes off. Then the sheets are pressed and pounded until they are soft and pliable.

clothes. Secondhand clothing imported from the United States and Europe is very popular. Colorful costumes consisting of long robes and dresses may be worn for ceremonies and holidays. Most Baganda men wear a *kanzu,* a long embroidered robe with long sleeves. A coat is sometimes worn over it. Many Ugandan women wear a wrap-around skirt with a blouse, or a busuti. The outfit resembles an English-style dress and was introduced by missionaries in the 1870s.

Food

Due to its fertile soil and abundant waters, Uganda has a wide variety of fruits and vegetables. Bananas, however, are the staple food of the Ugandan people. Bananas are very nourishing, and the Ugandan diet is fairly healthy, though not very varied. There are several types of bananas besides the familiar sweet, yellow banana. The large plantain banana is fried or mashed, or dried and ground into flour. Hard green bananas or plantains are made into the national dish called *matoke.* To prepare *matoke,* the cook peels and mashes bananas into a pulp, seasons the pulp and forms it into a ball, wraps it in banana leaves, and steams it. Bananas are also made into beer, wine, and an alcoholic drink called waragi. It is the national drink. Ugandans also eat many other tropical fruits and fresh vegetables, including passion fruit, oranges, mangoes, papayas, avocados, onions, tomatoes, and potatoes.

Two other staples of the Ugandan diet come from Lake Victoria— Nile perch and tilapia. Nile perch, which can weigh up to 300 pounds (136 kg), is usually served freshly cooked but sometimes smoked. The much smaller tilapia is almost always served freshly cooked. Another popular freshwater meal is the Nile crocodile. Some say it tastes like chicken.

Among wealthier Ugandans, beef stew is a mainstay. Goat and pork are also favorites. But the majority of people can't afford meat. They often eat peanuts and beans, important sources of protein, boiled and seasoned with ginger. Fried white ants and grasshoppers are a popular snack and also a source of protein. Corn is grown all over the country, and dishes prepared from it may be served at any meal. People also

TYPICAL DAILY DIET OF A CHILD IN UGANDA

Breakfast:	bread, margarine, fried banana, tea
Playtime:	bread, margarine
Lunch:	bread, margarine, piece of fruit
After school:	bottle of soda pop
Dinner:	fish twice a week, matoke (cooked banana), tea
Before bed:	tea

MATOKE

Matoke is the national dish in Uganda. It is usually made with plantains, which are harder than the bananas most Westerners eat. If you can't get plantains, you can use green bananas instead. Other fresh vegetables or meat may be added, if available. This recipe calls for simmering the matoke, though Ugandans usually put the mashed plantains back into their leaves and steam them. The finished dish looks and tastes something like a sweet mashed potato. It is often eaten on its own as a meal or along with a stew or piece of grilled meat.

4 plantains or green bananas

2 tablespoons lemon juice

1 tablespoon butter

1 onion, finely chopped

1 whole chili pepper, seeded and chopped

½ bunch fresh cilantro (coriander leaves)

2 cups canned vegetable or beef broth

1. Peel the bananas and slice into 1-inch rounds. Cover them in water mixed with the lemon juice and set aside.
2. Melt the butter on medium heat in a large saucepan. Fry the onions, chili pepper, and cilantro in the butter for 3 minutes.
3. Drain the banana slices. Add the bananas to pan, and cover with beef or vegetable stock. Bring to a boil, then simmer over low heat for 30 to 35 minutes, until bananas are tender.

Serves 4

make bread from millet or eat chapatis (Indian-style flatbread). In the drier, northern parts of the country, millet, sorghum, and cassava (a root vegetable that is ground into flour) are common food crops.

● Sports and Recreation

Sports are very popular in Uganda. The National Council of Sports, a Ugandan government agency, supports amateur sports organizations. Soccer (called football in countries outside the United States) is the most popular sport, followed by boxing, track and field, tennis, golf, motor sports, and cricket—a bat and ball game that came from Great Britain. The Acholi play a game called *undile* that is similar to field hockey.

Soccer is played at the amateur and professional level. Several African national teams compete in the Confederation of East and Central Africa Football Associations (CECAFA). The Uganda team, the Cranes, has won six titles in the CECAFA since it began in 1973, more than any other country. Teams also compete within Uganda for a national title. Championships are held annually in Kampala.

Ugandans have earned more fame in boxing than in any other sport. Idi Amin, for example, started out as a prize-winning boxer in his impoverished youth. The nation has won several medals at the Commonwealth Games (the Commonwealth is an association of former countries of the British Empire, including African and Asian countries as well as Canada, Australia, and others) and the Olympic Games. The sport is very popular among young people, who dream of using boxing to escape poverty and find a successful life.

Ugandans participate regularly in track-and-field events at the Olympics. They have had little success other than in 1972, when John Akii Bua won a gold medal for his Olympic record of 47.82 seconds in the 400-meter hurdles. Golf is played mostly by the rich, with tournaments throughout the year.

Other popular sports include mountain climbing and canoe racing. Adventure sports, such as white-water rafting at the source of the Nile, are popular with tourists. And with all the freshwater in the country, fishing is a favorite pastime in Uganda.

Many golf courses in Uganda have a rule that if a golf ball lands in a footprint made by a rhinoceros, the player may remove the ball without penalty. Rhinos weigh several tons and can leave a deep print.

THE ECONOMY

When Uganda gained its independence in 1962, it had one of the strongest economies in Africa. But two and a half decades of misman-agement and neglect by dictators—who usually spent huge amounts on the military and ignored the needs of average people—severely damaged its prosperity. Since the late 1980s, Uganda's economy has been recovering slowly and steadily.

The Museveni government has committed itself to careful budget-ing and spending as well as to increasing exports to bring in money. It has worked to encourage foreign investors to put money into Ugandan businesses. The government has introduced a privatization policy. Many businesses that had been run by the state, often inefficiently, were sold to private owners, who can pay closer attention to running them efficiently and effectively. The government owns certain utilities (public services such as electricity, water, and power), national parks, and the national bank. But by 1997, the majority of enterprises that had been owned by the state had been privatized. The government has also

made the nation more self-supporting, reducing the need for foreign aid. Uganda has created good relationships with international donors, who offer loans and economic advice. In the mid-1990s governments to whom Uganda owed money canceled much of Uganda's debt.

Uganda has begun to enjoy a stable economy due to these measures, though the country is poor. If the gross national income (or GNI, the total value of a nation's internal production and external income) were divided equally among all the nation's citizens in 2001, each citizen would have made about $280. Converted to purchasing power parity (PPP)—an indication of the value of goods and services a person could purchase regardless of their own currency's value—the average person would have made $1,460 that year. By contrast, the PPP per person worldwide was $7,160, and for an average person in sub-Saharan Africa as a whole, it was $1,710. In spite of an economy that has grown since the late 1980s, personal income in Uganda is only up to about the level it was in 1971, when Idi Amin came to power. However, much of the income in the Ugandan economy is not cash based and so does not show up in these statistics. Especially in rural areas, a large informal economy based on bartering (paying with goods and services instead of with cash) flourishes. Bartering gives Ugandans greater purchasing power than their cash income indicates.

Uganda's population is growing rapidly, putting further strain on the nation's resources. In addition to a high birth rate, Uganda is also taking in thousands of refugees who have fled civil wars in neighboring countries. In spite of these stresses, the people of Uganda do not face the starvation that many people in other poor nations face. Because of its ample resources of fertile soil and fresh water, Ugandans have enough to eat. Before British rule, most Ugandans were subsistence farmers and hunters, growing and catching the food they needed to survive. In modern times, the nation's economy continues to be driven largely by agriculture. Uganda has no problem growing enough food to feed its people, with enough left over to export to other countries.

◎ Agriculture

The largest and healthiest sector of Uganda's economy, agriculture consists of the production of crops and livestock as well as hunting, forestry, and fishing. Agriculture contributed about 42 percent of annual gross domestic product (GDP) in the early twenty-first century. The GDP is the value of all goods and services produced in a country during a given period. About 90 percent of money from exports comes from agriculture, and about 80 percent of the Ugandan labor force works in the agricultural sector. Agricultural output comes almost exclusively from small landholders. Only tea and sugar are produced on large estates.

The most important cash crop is coffee. Introduced by the British after World War II to bolster declining export revenues, coffee soon accounted for more than half the nation's export earnings and has remained its primary export crop. Uganda has tried to broaden its exports because dependence on coffee makes the nation's economy unstable, since the price of coffee varies a lot on the world market. In 1990 coffee accounted for more than 95 percent of the country's foreign exchange earnings. In 2000 that portion was about 57 percent. Coffee is grown mostly around the Lake Victoria basin.

Other principal cash crops include tea, cotton, corn, tobacco, sugarcane, vanilla, and cacao beans (from which cocoa is made). Before the introduction of coffee, cotton was the dominant cash crop. The production of cut flowers is also important. Main subsistence crops (crops people grow for their own food, not to sell) are plantains, cassava, sweet potatoes, millet, sorghum, corn, beans,

A Ugandan woman harvests a pineapple. Ugandan women grow 80 percent of food crops and 60 percent of export crops. Yet they own only 7 percent of the land.

peanuts, and rice. Cattle, goats, sheep, poultry, and other livestock are also raised. Freshwater fishing is also important, with fish farming a growing industry.

Services

The services sector contributes 39 percent of the annual GDP. The sector includes jobs in education, health care, retail, transportation, trade, and tourism. The most important economic area of this sector is trade. The principal sources of imports in the early twenty-first century were Kenya, the United Kingdom, Japan, and India. The main markets for exports were the United Kingdom, the Southern African Customs Union (a group of southern African countries), Kenya, and Singapore. The main export was coffee, and the main imports were petroleum products, road vehicles, medicinal and pharmaceutical products, and cereals.

Tourism is also included in services. In the 1960s and 1970s, it was the fastest-growing sector of the economy. It was expected to overtake the coffee industry as the nation's leading business. Tourism hit a peak in 1971, when more than 85,000 foreigners visited Uganda. But two decades of civil war and political turmoil changed that. Rebels damaged and looted hotels, killed wildlife herds, and blocked or damaged many national park roads. The current government recognizes the role tourism could play in its economy and has given high priority to restoring the tourism systems. The number of foreign visitors to Uganda grew in 2000 to more than 191,000 tourists. Most come from Kenya and Rwanda. Uganda's beautiful national park system is a popular tourist destination. Gorillas and chimpanzees are a major draw.

TOURISM IN UGANDA

Visitors are attracted to Uganda's national parks, game reserves, and animal sanctuaries, where a stunning variety of animals can be seen. As a result of neglect and poaching under the rule of Idi Amin, some animal species were drastically reduced in number. Others disappeared. Fighting destroyed hotels, roads, and other facilities, and violence discouraged visitors. President Museveni has made reviving the tourism sector a priority by promoting conservation and wildlife management, rebuilding hotels, and establishing programs to make it safer and easier to visit national parks and other tourist destinations. Museveni's efforts have had some successes, but tourism remains a resource that has not been tapped to its full potential.

◉ Industry

Chipping in 19 percent of the GDP, industry is Uganda's third-largest economic sector. Industry includes manufacturing, construction, power, and mining. Manufacturing contributes 9 percent of the GDP. It is an area that was particularly damaged during the Amin regime. Before Amin, Uganda had a large manufacturing base, but after thousands of Asian business owners were expelled, the businesses were given to people who had no business knowledge. By the end of the Amin regime, manufacturing was on the brink of collapse. In the twenty-first century, the most significant manufacturing activities are food processing, brewing, vehicle assembly, and the production of textiles, cement, soap, fertilizers, paper products, metal products, shoes, paints, matches, and batteries.

Uganda's power consumption is growing at a rate of about 20 percent a year. Its energy is created primarily through hydroelectric power (power created by rushing water harnessed by dams). Uganda generates only about two-thirds of its energy needs. Imports

Factory workers in Kampala assemble televisions from parts made in India. For more information about manufacturing in Uganda, visit www.vgsbooks.com.

of fuel account for the rest. Plans are under way to expand hydroelectric production, and the government hopes to export electricity to Kenya, Tanzania, and Rwanda.

Uganda has a great variety of mineral resources, including gold, copper, diamonds, coal, and oil. In the 1970s, however, the mines were closed when the owners were forced to leave the country. So mining has made little contribution to the GDP. Uganda has plans for the nation's largest copper mine to be privatized and reopened. Uganda is believed to possess the world's second-largest deposit of gold, which is being exploited again. Limestone is also mined. As of 1999, cobalt (a strong, magnetic metal) is being produced. Uganda also has reserves of iron ore, magnetite, tin, tungsten, beryllium, bismuth, asbestos, graphite, phosphate, and tantalite.

Transportation and Telecommunications

Like so much of Uganda's society, the nation's transportation and telecommunications systems were in shambles by 1986. The Museveni government realized that rebuilding them would be crucial to the nation's economy. In particular, improving the road and rail systems would aid the moving of products to markets throughout the country.

Uganda has almost 17,000 miles (27,000 km) of roads. About 1,100 miles (1,800 km) of them are paved. Most roads start from Kampala. The condition of the road system has been greatly improved since 1986, and new roads have been constructed. In 2000 there were eight vehicles for every 1,000 Ugandans. Many families own at least one bicycle, and in small cities, bicycle-taxis carry people short distances. Traffic moves on the left-hand side of the road, as in Great Britain.

In protectorate times, the British built an 871-mile (1,400-km) railway that linked Uganda to the Kenyan seaport of Mombasa. It was a key line for Uganda because access to this major port provides access to the world economy. By the late 1980s, the line was unusable and in desperate need of repair. The NRM has repaired this and other lines throughout the country. It has also built a line from Kampala to Port Bell, Tanzania, providing an alternate outlet to the sea. Additionally, a $20 million project is under way to establish a direct rail link between Kampala and Johannesburg, South Africa, also on the sea. Uganda has about 800 miles (1,287 km) of rail lines.

Uganda has an international airport at Entebbe as well as twenty-six other regional airports. The national airline is the state-owned Uganda Airlines.

The telephone system is described by the Central Intelligence Agency (CIA) of the United States as "seriously inadequate." About 61,700 telephone main lines were in use in 2000, about 2.8 per 1,000 people. (More than 100,000 were in use before Idi Amin seized power.) About 56,400 people use mobile phones. About 60,000 personal computers are in use, about 2.7 per 1,000 people, with about 25,000 Internet users.

◎ The Future

When Yoweri Museveni was sworn in as president on January 26, 1986, he said his NRM government represented not "a mere change of guards, but a fundamental change." Indeed, since the NRM has been in power, peace has been established in most parts of the country for the first time in years. Uganda's constitution makes democracy the basis for government. Social and economic systems have been vastly improved. Ethnic tensions have eased. Careful government spending, privatization of previously state-owned enterprises, and a reinvigorated export market have created a stronger economy. Tourism has increased. One of the greatest signs of hope for the future is the high attendance rate of children going to primary school and building a more educated society. All of these improvements bring welcome stability to a nation that has endured civil war, terror, corruption, and devastating poverty since independence. President Museveni himself can stand as a symbol of this stability, as he has been in power for longer than any previous leader of Uganda.

However, Uganda's peace is fragile and the future is far from certain. The country faces many challenges from its position in an unstable and conflict-torn region of the world. Some argue that Museveni has not controlled corruption in government and that his forceful foreign policy has deteriorated relations with neighboring countries. Many believe that in spite of the relatively peaceful period, Uganda remains a deeply divided society that could easily unravel at the end of his presidency. Guerrilla rebel groups, such as the Lord's Resistance Army, continue to operate in parts of the country, so the threat of violence looms. Ugandans hope and work for the peace and stability to continue. And they hope too that, as they work together to tap their country's great potential, more prosperity lies ahead.

A CEREMONY OF FORGIVENESS

An age-old ceremony of forgiveness is being used in northern Uganda as one of the strategies to create a peaceful future. The LRA and other violent rebel groups have terrorized the area since 1987. Tens of thousands of young people, mostly under thirteen, have been abducted, the boys forced to kill and the girls "married" to rebel commanders. In 2000 Uganda offered amnesty (legal forgiveness for people who surrender), and thousands of rebels surrendered. Many of the returning men and women had been abducted years ago, then had returned to murder, mutilate, and steal from their own people. They now seek to come back home. Communities mostly welcome them back, but the path of healing is difficult on both sides. As part of the healing, former rebels make a statement of apology. In a traditional ceremony, they then dip their bare right feet in a freshly cracked egg. The egg is a symbol of innocent life and the return to the way the people used to be.

Timeline

CA. 290,000–140,000 B.C.	The first humans *(Homo sapiens)* live in East Africa.
A.D. 1000	The first states, including Bunyoro-Kitara, form in Uganda.
1350	Bunyoro-Kitara has a multilevel government led by a king.
CA. 1400s	The Buganda and Ankole kingdoms are established.
1636–1663	Buganda doubles and redoubles its size, becoming the most powerful kingdom in the region.
CA. 1830	The kingdom of Toro is established.
1844	Arab ivory and slave traders reach Uganda, introducing guns to the region.
1858	John Hanning Speke reaches Lake Victoria at Jinja and claims that the lake is the headwaters of the Nile River.
1874	Henry M. Stanley confirms that Lake Victoria is the source of the Nile.
1877	Protestant missionaries arrive in Buganda to convert Baganda.
1879	Catholic missionaries arrive in Buganda.
1892	Protestant and Catholic converts begin fighting in Buganda. British and German imperialists join the fight, with the British and Protestants eventually defeating the Catholics and Germans.
1894	Great Britain establishes Uganda as a protectorate on June 18. Several counties within Bunyoro-Kitara are awarded to Buganda.
1900	Britain signs the Uganda Agreement with Buganda, giving Buganda privileged status.
1904	Cultivation of cotton as a cash crop in Uganda begins.
1907	Banyoro living in the "lost counties" revolt, forcing many Baganda chiefs out of Bunyoro.
1914	Britain controls most of Uganda.
1933	Britain signs the Banyoro Agreement.
1939–1945	During World War II, 77,131 Ugandans serve alongside the British.
1949	Baganda separatists riot, demanding—among other things—their own representatives in local government.
1952	Sir Andrew Cohen becomes governor of Uganda and begins taking steps to create a united, independent Uganda in which Buganda is a province without special privileges.
1953	Cohen has King Freddie deported to Great Britain, sparking the kabaka crisis.

1955   The Progressive Party (PP), one of Uganda's first political parties, is formed.

1960   The Uganda People's Congress (UPC), led by Milton Obote, is formed.

1962   Uganda gains its independence on October 9. Obote becomes prime minister.

1966   Obote promotes Idi Amin to army chief of state.

1967   Obote establishes a new constitution that grants the president sweeping powers.

1971   After hearing of an Obote order to have him arrested, Amin topples Obote in a coup and declares himself president.

1972   Amin orders all Israelis and Asians out of the country.

1978   Amin invades Tanzania and annexes a section of it.

1979   Tanzania, aided by Ugandan exiles, invades Uganda and forces Amin to flee the country. Yusufu Lule is installed as president, but he is soon replaced by Godfrey Binaisa.

1981   Obote becomes president after elections.

1985   Obote orders the arrest of Brigadier Basilio Okello, who responds by toppling Obote in a coup. Obote flees to Zambia and is replaced by Okello.

1986   The National Resistance Army (NRA), led by Yoweri Museveni, takes Kampala and installs Museveni as president. Several rebel groups join forces against the new government.

1987   The Holy Spirit movement rebellion is suppressed. The Holy Spirit movement regroups as the Lord's Resistance Army (LRA).

1993   Museveni restores the traditional kings as ceremonial positions.

1995   A new constitution legalizes political parties but maintains a ban on political activity. Museveni accuses Sudan of supporting the LRA.

1996   Museveni is elected president in Uganda's first direct presidential election.

1998   Uganda intervenes in a civil war in the Democratic Republic of Congo.

2001   Museveni wins another term in office.

2002   Ugandan troops capture all four main bases of the LRA in southern Sudan.

2003   LRA activity surges again. Many Baganda demonstrate for semiautonomous status for their kingdom. Idi Amin dies in exile in Saudi Arabia.

2004   The LRA and the Ugandan government hold their first face-to-face talks in December, but no solution is reached.

2005   Demonstrators peacefully protest against plans to allow Museveni to run for a third term as president in 2006.

COUNTRY NAME Republic of Uganda

AREA 93,066 square miles (241,040 sq. km)

MAIN LANDFORMS mountain regions, Central Plateau, Great Rift Valley, Mount Elgon, Imateng Mountains, Ruwenzori Mountains, Virunga Mountains, Dodoth Hills, Labwor Hills

HIGHEST POINT Margherita Peak on Mount Stanley, 16,762 feet (5,109 m)

LOWEST POINT Lake Albert, about 2,000 feet (600 m) above sea level

MAJOR RIVERS Victorial Nile, Albert Nile, Katonga, Semliki, Zoka, Achwa, Pager, Dopeth-Okok, Mpologoma

ANIMALS mountain gorillas, galago, chimpanzees, monkeys, elephants, African buffalo, antelope, zebras, giraffes, lions, leopards, hyenas, rock hyrax, black rhinoceros, hippopotamuses, crocodiles, lizards, frogs, toads, tiger fish, Nile perch, tilapia, crowned crane, bulbul, mousebird, sparrows, starlings, sunbirds, herons, storks, kingfishers, vultures, hawks, eagles, falcons

CAPITAL CITY Kampala

OTHER MAJOR CITIES Jinja, Entebbe, Mbale, Masaka, Gulu

OFFICIAL LANGUAGE English

MONETARY UNIT Uganda shilling. 100 cents = 1 shilling.

UGANDAN CURRENCY

The Uganda shilling, abbreviated as Ush, is made up of 100 cents. Coins in denominations of 1, 2, 5, and 10 shillings are in circulation, but due to inflation, these coins have little real value and are rarely used. Only paper money is in regular use. Banknotes are available in denominations of 5, 10, 20, 50, 100, 200, 500, 1,000, 5,000, and 10,000 Ush.

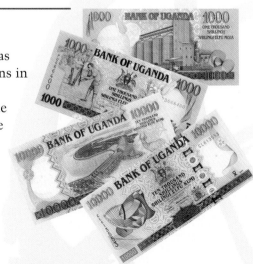

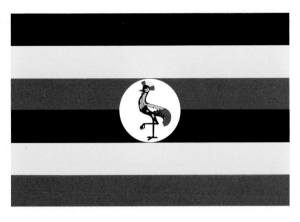

The Republic of Uganda has a colorful flag that features the national bird, the crowned crane, in a white circle on a background of six stripes alternating in black, yellow, and red. Black represents the people of the country, yellow represents sunshine, and red represents unity. The flag, created by Grace Ibingira, was adopted on the date of independence, October 9, 1962.

The national anthem of Uganda, written and composed by George Wilberforce Kakoma, is called "Pearl of Africa." It was adopted on the date of independence, October 9, 1962.

Pearl of Africa
Oh Uganda! may God uphold thee,
We lay our future in thy hand.
United, free,
For liberty
Together we'll always stand.

Oh Uganda! the land of freedom.
Our love and labor we give,
And with neighbors all
At our country's call
In peace and friendship we'll live.

Oh Uganda! the land that feeds us
By sun and fertile soil grown.
For our own dear land,
We'll always stand,
The Pearl of Africa's Crown.

For a link to an opportunity to listen to the national anthem of Uganda, go to www.vgsbooks.com.

Famous People

IDI AMIN (CA. 1928–2003) One of the world's most notorious dictators, Amin was born in Kampala and grew up uneducated and poor. He joined the army in 1944 to escape hunger, he said, and he was the Ugandan heavyweight boxing champion from 1951 to 1960. In 1971 he seized control of Uganda. His reign was marked by mass deportations, violence, fear, and poverty. Amin is blamed for the death of about 500,000 people during his eight-year regime. His eccentric behavior, including boasting of cannibalism (eating human flesh), drew international attention. He had five wives and dozens of children. After he was overthrown in 1979, Amin flew to Libya and later settled in Saudi Arabia, where he died in 2003.

ELIZABETH BAGAYA (b. 1936) Known as Princess Elizabeth of Toro, Bagaya was born into the Toro royal family in western Uganda. She studied law at Oxford University in Great Britain, the first Ugandan woman to become a lawyer. She became an international fashion model, appearing on the cover of *Vogue* magazine, as well as acting in several motion pictures. Idi Amin appointed her ambassador to the United Nations in 1971, then foreign minister in 1974, but he dismissed her when she fell from his favor. She lived in exile until 1986. Under President Museveni, she was the ambassador to the United States from 1986 to 1988.

OKOT P'BITEK (1931–1982) Okot p'Bitek, an Acholi, is one of Uganda's most famous writers of folklore, satirical poems, and songs. In his youth, he played for the Uganda national soccer team. He published his first novel, *Lak Tar (White Teeth)*—about a young Acholi man who must work away from home to earn money for a bridewealth—in 1953. His book *Song of Lawino* (1966) is a story written in traditional Acholi verse. He was born in Gulu, in northern Uganda.

JOSE CHAMELEON (b. 1980) Perhaps Uganda's most up-and-coming young pop music star, Jose Chameleon took four awards at the newly established Pearl of Africa Music Awards in 2003, including Artist of the Year and Song of the Year. In 2004 he released his album *Mambo Bado* and helped organize the Big Free-Entry Hope Concert, a benefit concert held to encourage peace in conflict-torn northern Uganda.

APOLO KAGWA (1869–1927) Kagwa, born in Busoga, served as the prime minister of Buganda from 1890 to 1926 and was the leading figure in establishing semiautonomous status for Buganda under British rule. He was also a leader of the Protestant faction in the civil wars of the Baganda people from 1888 to 1892. He was an author and wrote *The Customs of the Baganda People.*

SPECIOZA WANDIRA KAZIBWE (b. 1955) Kazibwe was the vice president of Uganda from 1994 to 2003, the first woman vice president in all of Africa. A medical doctor, Kazibwe was born in the Iganga District in eastern

Uganda and earned her degree in medicine from Makerere University. In 1986 she began serving in the government and said she was dedicated to "advancing women, reducing poverty and the high level of illiteracy, and promoting social justice." In 2003 Dr. Kazibwe resigned from the vice presidency to study for a PhD in medicine at Harvard University in the United States.

PHILLY BONGOLE LUTAAYA (1951–1989) Lutaaya was a music star in Uganda. His hit album, *Born in Africa*, made him Uganda's top popular musician of the 1980s. By the end of that decade, he revealed that he had AIDS and used his celebrity to educate youth about how to protect themselves from the disease. In a talk to students, he said, "Let us do our best to have a virus-free young generation. It's easy to avoid getting the virus. I beseech you, please be careful in the way you handle yourselves. We need you." Uganda's nationwide AIDS awareness campaign was due in part to his efforts.

YOWERI MUSEVENI (b. 1944) The president of Uganda from 1986 until the present, Museveni was born in the Ankole region of Uganda and received his university education in Tanzania. In 1980 his party was defeated in elections that he said had been rigged. He then formed the National Resistance Army that brought him to power in 1986. He was returned to office in 1996 in Uganda's first direct presidential election and was reelected in 2001. His government brought relative peace and prosperity to a country that had been plagued by violence and poverty for decades.

MAGID MUSISI (b. CA. 1966) Musisi is the only Ugandan soccer player to have played professionally in Europe. He started playing professional soccer in Uganda in 1986 and became the first Ugandan to score one hundred league goals. In 1992 Musisi went to Europe, where he played for a French club and later two clubs in Turkey, becoming the top scorer at all three clubs. He lives in Kampala.

JOHN HANNING SPEKE (1827–1864) Born in Devon, Great Britain, Speke was a member of Richard Burton's 1855 expedition to explore East Africa, where he was almost killed in an attack. On his next trip with Burton, in 1858, Speke discovered the source of the Nile. He later returned to Lake Victoria to map the river but was halted by an outbreak of local warfare. Speke actually was not a very good geographer. Skeptics pointed out, for instance, that by his calculations, the Nile flowed uphill. He was right, however, that he had found the source of the river. Speke was killed by his own gun while hunting, on the day he was to debate Burton publicly.

Sights to See

BWINDI IMPENETRABLE NATIONAL PARK Bwindi, like Mgahinga, is home to the rare mountain gorilla. Bwindi lies on the border with Congo. Much of the park has dense forest and steep slopes, which gives it its name—"impenetrable." Gorilla tracking, a difficult but worthwhile activity, is done with a guide. Only sixteen gorilla-tracking permits are available per day, to protect the gorillas from too much human disturbance.

KASUBI ROYAL TOMBS Located southwest of Kampala, this site is the resting place of four kings of Buganda. Items such as spears, shields, and photographs lie in front of each king's platform. Four women sit inside, two on each side of the burial house, representing the widows of the kings.

MGAHINGA GORILLA NATIONAL PARK Established in 1991, Mgahinga is one of Uganda's newest national parks. It lies in the extreme southwestern corner of the country. One-half of the world's remaining mountain gorillas make their home here, though they sometimes cross the border into Congo. The park contains three extinct volcanoes and is covered by rain forest.

MURCHISON FALLS The falls lie in the Murchison Falls National Park. At the falls, the 160-foot-wide (49-m-wide) Nile River squeezes through a 23-foot (7-m) slot in the rocks and drops 141 feet (43 m). The thundering rush of water creates a mist and rainbow that are virtually constant. The rest of the park contains lush plant life and vast animal life.

NATIONAL THEATRE Situated in Kampala, the National Theatre is the venue for annual music and drama festivals and is the headquarters for the Uganda Theatrical Groups Association. On the grounds behind the theater is the Arts and Crafts Village, where artwork is displayed and sold.

QUEEN ELIZABETH NATIONAL PARK Queen Elizabeth National Park lies in the west near Lakes Edward and George. Once one of the richest parks for wildlife, it was damaged during the civil wars of the 1960s, 1970s, and early 1980s. It is steadily regaining its vast animal life and is one of the best places in the world to see hippos.

RUWENZORI MOUNTAINS NATIONAL PARK These magnificent mountains, though they lie on the equator, are capped with snow and ice because their peaks are so high. The highest peak, Margherita, rises 16,762 feet (5,109 m). The land is constantly shrouded by mist.

SESE ISLANDS These eighty-four islands in Lake Victoria are a popular tourist spot, as the islands offer a relaxing and peaceful visit. Popular activities there are bird-watching and boating.

UGANDA NATIONAL MUSEUM The Uganda National Museum is in Kampala. It is home to many of the nation's treasured historical arts and crafts, as well as fossils and cultural artifacts.

bridewealth: a set of gifts that a Ugandan man must give the parents of a woman he wishes to marry

busuti: a blouse and skirt that many Ugandan women wear that resembles a nineteenth-century English-style dress. The busuti was introduced to Ugandans by missionaries in the 1870s.

cash crops: crops grown to be sold for cash. The primary cash crops in Uganda are coffee, cotton, and tea.

coup: the sudden and sometimes violent overthrow of a government

equator: an imaginary circle around the earth that is equally distant from the North Pole and the South Pole, and which divides the Northern Hemisphere and the Southern Hemisphere

galago: also known as bush babies, these nocturnal primates have large eyes, a long tail, and long hind limbs that help them leap with great agility. They are the smallest primates in Africa.

Great Rift Valley: a series of massive valleys that extends about 4,500 miles (7,200 km) through much of Asia and Africa

gross domestic product (GDP): a measure of the total value of goods and services producted within a country in a year

gross national income (GNI): the total value of production within a nation plus income to the country from the rest of the world

guerrilla: a person who engages in radical and irregular warfare, especially as part of a rebel group

imperialist: a nation or person who tries on behalf of a nation to extend the power of that nation by gaining control over new territories

kabaka: the king of Buganda

kanzu: a long robe with long sleeves that most Baganda men wear

matoke: green bananas peeled, mashed, and seasoned, then steamed in the banana leaves. Matoke is known as the national dish of Uganda.

poaching: the illegal catching or killing of animals

protectorate: a country or state that is ruled by a foreign one. Uganda was a protectorate of Great Britain from 1894 to 1962. The land rights of native people in a protectorate are recognized; in a colony, they are not.

purchasing power parity (PPP): conversion of the value of goods and services to international dollars, making it possible to compare how much similar goods and services cost to the residents of different countries. Statistics such as GDP and GNI are based on PPP calculations.

referendum: a popular vote on a measure

separatism: a movement for the separation (autonomy) of one part of a country from the rest of the country. Many Baganda are separatists.

Briggs, Philip. *Uganda: The Bradt Travel Guide.* Chalfont St. Peter, UK: Bradt Publications, 1998.
This travel guide has short sections on Uganda's geography, history, and the people, but it is most valuable for its sections on plant and animal life.

British Broadcasting Corporation. *BBC News.*
http://news.bbc.co.uk/ (May 9, 2005).
This website is an extensive international news source. It contains political and cultural news, as well as country profiles, and is updated regularly.

Byrnes, Rita M. *Uganda: A Country Study.* Washington, DC: Federal Research Division, Library of Congress, 1992.
This publication offers a thorough study of Uganda, including extensive coverage of history up to 1990, society and culture, economy, and government and politics.

Central Intelligence Agency. "The World Factbook—Uganda." The World Factbook. 2003.
http://www.cia.gov/cia/publications/factbook/geos/ug.html (May 9, 2005).
This website page provides a general profile of Uganda, produced by the U.S. CIA. The profile includes brief summaries of the nation's geography, people, government, economy, communications, transportation, and military.

The Europa World Yearbook, 2002. London: Europa Publications Limited, 2002.
This is an annual publication that includes coverage of Uganda's recent history, economy, and government, as well as a wealth of statistics on population, employment, trade, and more. A short directory of offices and organizations is also included.

Fitzpatrick, Mary, Nick Ray, and Tom Parkinson. *East Africa.* Melbourne, AUS: Lonely Planet, 2003.
A guidebook that covers Tanzania, Kenya, Rwanda, and Burundi as well as Uganda, this book offers in-depth coverage of the countries. Useful sections on history, geography, ecology, flora and fauna, culture, and more are offered as well.

Gakwandi, Arthur. *Uganda Pocket Facts.* Kampala: Fountain Publishers, 1999.
This country guide provides information on the history, culture, economy, and politics of Uganda.

Lacy, Marc. "Victims of Uganda Atrocities Follow a Path of Forgiveness." *New York Times,* April 18, 2005.
This article explores African traditions of forgiveness being used to reintegrate people who were part of the violent LRA cult in northern Uganda back into society. In many cases, the cult members had been stolen as children from the very places they are coming back to.

The Monitor Publications Ltd. *The Monitor.* 2005.
http://www.monitor.co.ug/ (May 9, 2005)
This is the website for the *Monitor,* Uganda's most important independent newspaper. It reports news, entertainment, sports, and other stories, and is updated regularly.

Selected Bibliography

Ofcansky, Thomas P. *Uganda: Tarnished Pearl of Africa.* Boulder, CO: Westview Press, 1996.
This book is one in a series called Nations of the Modern World. It provides an overview of Uganda, focusing on its history and how that has shaped the country, especially its society, culture, and the economy.

Orizio, Riccardo. *Talk of the Devil: Encounters with Seven Dictators.* Translated by Avril Bardoni. New York: Walker & Company, 2003.
Orizio is an Italian journalist who sought out and interviewed ex-dictators around the world. The section on Idi Amin, who spoke with Orizio not long before Amin died in Saudi Arabia, is fascinating and informative.

"PRB 2004 World Population Data Sheet." *Population Reference Bureau (PRB).* 2004.
http://www.prb.org (September 1, 2004).
This annual statistics sheet provides a wealth of population, demographic, and health statistics for Uganda and almost all countries in the world.

Raffaele, Paul. "Uganda, the Horror." *Smithsonian*, February 2005.
This article covers what has been called the world's "largest neglected humanitarian emergency," the plight of children in northern Uganda, terrorized by the Lord's Resistance Army. Photos of the lives of young people who have escaped or been rescued from the LRA accompany the text.

Reader, John. *Africa.* Washington, DC: National Geographic, 2001.
This large, photo-illustrated volume is a companion to the eight-hour PBS series *Africa.*

———. *Africa: A Biography of the Continent.* New York: A. A. Knopf, 1998.
This book is a history of humanity in the continent of Africa.

Spectrum Guide to Uganda. New York: Interlink Books, 1998.
This travel guide has thorough sections on Uganda's history, flora, fauna, culture, economy, the land, and much more.

The Statesman's Yearbook: The Politics, Cultures, and Economics of the World, 2002. New York: St. Martin's Press, 2002.
This annual publication provides concise information on Uganda's history, climate, government, economy, and culture, including relevant statistics.

U.S. Department of State Bureau of Public Affairs. "Background Note: Uganda." *U.S. Department of State.* 2003.
http://www.state.gov/r/pa/ei/bgn/2963.htm (May 9, 2005).
This website page provides a general profile of Uganda, produced by the U.S. Department of State. The profile includes brief summaries of the nation's geography, people, government and politics, and economy.

Allen, John, and Tamra Orr. *Idi Amin.* San Diego: Blackbirch, 2003.
This is a biography of Uganda's brutal dictator Idi Amin.

Barlas, Robert. *Uganda.* New York: Marshall Cavendish, 2000.
This book offers an introduction to the geography, history, government, economy, people, and culture of Uganda.

Further Reading and Websites

Blauer, Ettagale, and Jason Lauré. *Uganda.* **New York: Children's Press, 1997.**
Part of the Enchantment of the World series, this book describes the geography, history, culture, industry, and people of Uganda.

De Temmerman, Els. *Aboke Girls: Children Abducted in Northern Uganda.* **Kampala, Uganda: Fountain Publishers, 2001.**
About 130 girls were abducted from a boarding school in Aboke in 1996. This book is about these girls and the child soldiers in northern Uganda and one woman's efforts to rescue them.

Hansen, Joyce. *African Princess.* **New York: Hyperion Books, 2004.**
Paintings and photos illustrate the lives of six royal women from Africa's history, including Princess Elizabeth of Toro from Uganda. Her fascinating life story, so far, is covered.

Isegawa, Moses. *Abyssinian Chronicles.* **New York: Knopf, 2000.**
This is a novel about life in twentieth-century Uganda. It is the story of Mugezi, beginning with his birth in a rural village in the early 1960s to his emigration to the Netherlands in 1985.

Jackson, Dave. *Assassins in the Cathedral.* **Minneapolis: Bethany House, 1998.**
This is the story of Yacobo, who has been asked by Bishop Kivengere to help him with some university research. But when Idi Amin's soldiers attack and kill Kivengere, Yacobo and his family have to worry about their own survival.

Langley, Andrew. *Explorers on the Nile.* **Morristown, NJ: Silver Burdett, 1981.**
This book discusses four explorers of the Nile River, including John Hanning Speke, Samuel Baker, David Livingstone, and Henry M. Stanley.

Mann, Kenny. *Zenj, Buganda: East Africa.* **Parsippany, NJ: Dillon Press, 1997.**
This book is a study of the history, legends, and life of people of two areas of East Africa, including the kingdom of Buganda.

Nabwire, Constance, and Bertha Vining Montgomery. *Cooking the East African Way.* **Minneapolis: Lerner Publications Company, 2002.**
This cultural cookbook features recipes from the East African countries of Uganda, Kenya, Ethiopia, and Tanzania. It also looks at the culture, history, and land of the region, and includes maps and photos.

Okurut, Mary Karooro, ed. *A Woman's Voice: An Anthology of Short Stories by Ugandan Women.* **Kampala, Uganda: Femrite Publishing, 1998.**
This book is a collection of short stories by Ugandan women authors.

Piwang, Catherine Mudibo. *A Visit from the Leopard: Memories of a Ugandan Childhood.* **New York: Pippin Press, 2000.**
This is the story of Mbiro, who was named for the swiftly racing leopard, and her childhood experiences in the Ugandan village of Butangasi.

Serwadda, W. Moses. *Songs and Stories from Uganda.* **Transcribed and edited by Hewitt Pantaleoni. Illustrated by Leo and Diane Dillon. New York: Crowell, 1974.**
This is a collection of thirteen songs accompanied by stories retold from Ugandan folklore.

Uganda Embassy.
http://www.ugandaembassy.com
The website of the Uganda Embassy has information on the government and country of Uganda.

www.vgsbooks.com
http://www.vgsbooks.com
Visit www.vgsbooks.com, the home page of the Visual Geography Series®, which is updated regularly. You can get linked to all sorts of useful online information, including geographical, historical, demographic, cultural, and economic websites. The www.vgsbooks.com site is a great resource for late-breaking news and statistics.

Matovu, Moses, 51
Mbale, 19, 36–37, 44, 68
media, 50
mineral resources, 4, 14, 63
mining, 62, 63
mountains, 9, 10, 12, 68; Alexandra
    Peak, 10; Margherita Peak, 10;
    Mount Elgon, 10; Mount Stanley,
    10, 68
Museveni, Yoweri, 7, 32, 33–35, 48,
    67, 71; reforms, 38, 39, 42, 44, 47,
    50, 65
music, 48, 49, 50–51
musical instruments, 46–47, 50, 51,
    80
Musisi, Magid, 71
Mutesa II (Edward Frederick
    Walugembe, also Kabaka Freddie),
    27, 28, 29, 66

national anthem, 69
national parks, 15, 16, 58, 62;
    Budongo Forest Reserve, 12;
    Bwindi Impenetrable National
    Park, 17, 72; Lake Mburo National
    Park, 4–5, 72, 80; Mgahinga
    Gorilla National Park, 72, 80;
    Murchison Falls National Park, 13,
    72; Queen Elizabeth National
    Park, 51, 72; Ruwenzori
    Mountains National Park, 72
National Resistance Army (NRA).
    See antigovernment groups
National Resistance Movement
    (NRM) 33, 35
natural resources, 4, 14

Obote, Milton, 28, 29, 30, 32–33, 67

p'Bitek, Okot, 52, 70
performing arts, 52
plate tectonics, 12
population, 18, 19, 36, 40
population growth. See domestic
    challenges
poverty. See domestic challenges

recipe (matoke), 56
religion, 46, 47–48
rivers, 8, 13–14, 68; Katonga, 14, 68;

Nile, 9, 12, 13–14, 19, 23, 68

services, 61–62
Speke, John Hanning, 23, 66, 71
sports and recreation, 46, 56–57
syncretism. See religion

telecommunications, 65
topography, 9–10, 12–13
tourism, 13, 14, 57, 61, 62, 65
transportation, 64–65

Uganda: boundaries, location, and
    size, 4, 8–9; currency, 68; flag, 69;
    flora and fauna, 4, 8, 15–16, 68;
    government, 35, 65; maps, 6, 11;
    national anthem, 69; official name,
    4, 8, 68
Uganda National Liberation Army,
    31, 32

women, 34, 35, 38–39, 40, 41, 61;
    AIDS, 42; authors, 53–54; Bagaya,
    Elizabeth, 70; female genital
    mutilation (FGM), 42–43;
    Kazibwe, Specioza Wandira, 34,
    38, 70; motherhood, 40; Titi, 51.
    See also marriage
World War I, 26
World War II, 26, 27, 60, 66

Captions for photos appearing on cover and chapter openers:

Cover: Mount Muhavura, one of the three extinct volcanoes in Mgahinga Gorilla National Park in southwestern Uganda, towers over terraced farmland.

pp. 4–5 Water birds gather at the shore of one of the four lakes in Lake Mburo National Park in south central Uganda.

pp. 8–9 Lake Victoria, seen here on the horizon, surrounds the rich green forested hills of Buggala Island, one of Uganda's Sese Islands.

pp. 36–37 Pedestrians and bicyclists make their way in Mbale's shopping district. Mbale, situated at the base of Mount Elgon in eastern Uganda, has a population of more than 70,000 people.

pp. 46–47 Ugandan girls perform a traditional dance accompanied by a group of boys playing a variety of drums.

pp. 58–59 The Owen Falls Dam harnesses the power of water flowing from Lake Victoria into the Victoria Nile River in eastern Uganda.

Photo Acknowledgments
The images in this book are used with the permission of: © Paul Joynson-Hicks/Art Directors, pp. 4–5, 8–9, 13, 15, 18, 36–37, 46–47, 51, 53, 54 (bottom), 58–59, 61; © XNR Productions, pp. 6, 11; © Ray Wood/Panos Pictures, p. 10; © James P. Rowan, p. 16; © Claudia Adams/Root Resources, p. 17; © Jason Laure, pp. 22, 32; Library of Congress, p. 26 (LC-USZ62-40555); © Terrence Spencer/Time Life Pictures/Getty Images, p. 28; © AP/Wide World Photos, p. 31; © Crispin Hughes/Panos Pictures, p. 33; © Ted Farrington/Root Resources, p. 39; © Sean Sprague/Panos Pictures, pp. 41, 43; © David Lees/Time Life Pictures/Getty Images, p. 49; Courtesy Picador Pan Macmillan Publishing, p. 54 (top); © Paul Joynson-Hicks/Laure Communications, p. 63; Audrius Tomonis—www.banknotes.com, p. 68.

Front cover: © Michael S. Lewis/CORBIS. Back cover: NASA.